About the Author

Jarvis James was reared and resides in St. Louis Missouri, with his lovely wife Regina L. James. They have one wonderful daughter, Beloved James. He strives daily to consistently apply the standards set forth in this book to his own life while he instructs and guides others in doing the same. Jarvis James is a pastor, writer, avid chess player, professional motivational speaker and leader of a movement fueled with passion to take back our communities through character education.

Jarvis James

Bricks for Building Character

Essential Values for Developing the 21st Century Youth

Books currently in print include:

Bricks For Building Character
Keep Your "But" Out Of God's Business
Raise 'Em High

To Order More Copies of this book or others
Contact Jarvis James
gogopreacher@hotmail.com
Be sure to include your name, phone number and number of books you desire.
Thank you for your patronage.

Bricks for Building Character™. Copyright © 2011 by Jarvis A. James.
All rights reserved.

blurb

blurb.com

This book is dedicated to my daughter Beloved and to all future generations that want to take the challenge of becoming better people in this world through character education.

Contents

Introduction... *A Work in Progress*		1
How to Use This Book		3

Good Values   Opposite

Good Values	Opposite	
Respect	Disrespect	5
Honesty	Lying	19
Fairness	Cheating	29
Courage	Coward	41
Persistence	Lazy	53
Excellence	Mediocrity	65
Passion	Uncaring	77
Leadership	Slacker	89
Service	User	99
Liberty	Imprisonment	111
Love	Hate	123
Confidence	Boastful	133
Teamwork	Selfish	143
Forgiveness	Revenge	155

Bricks for Building Character

Introduction.....A Work in Progress

Bricks for Building Character is a book that strategically exposes the set of values that are essential to developing the character of young readers and the tireless humanitarian spirits developing the youth of today. The lessons learned ahead may or may not yield immediate results, but as these young people grow older they are certain to call upon these core values to direct the path of their lives.

It is difficult for everyone to agree on what the core values are. Of all the sources that can be tapped for what one needs to know to live a healthy life; it's proven that the core values of the Bible and this country have fueled the massive success of they that have taken them on.

Foundational values are sorely missing in many homes, schools and communities that will be instrumental in marking the future success for today's youth. This is a tragedy because the foundation of any structure must be laid first before anything can be built upon it. There are strong foundational values that successful people have applied throughout history that assures massive results for the good of the world. In this book just as in life, if you build your life on good values you will have a solid foundation for good permanent results. Yet on the opposite side, one can build their lives on bad principles and have an equally strong foundation to end up with bad permanent results. These values and their opposites are exposed in a simple yet riveting way that all youth can understand and apply here in Bricks for Building Character. The thought provoking explanations of each core value and its opposing habit or principle empowers youth with the choice of the path they want to pursue in life.

Introduction... A Work in Progress

The way people get better is to discover and to fully develop what is on the inside of them. This book is a practical guide to enable youth and those involved with youth, to learn more about the pillars of inside stuff that helps us deal with the outside stuff. As youth explore these paths they will become instantly engaged in their own development. Bricks for Building Character will take them on a journey as they investigate the value and its opposite principle, identify its real effect on others' lives through Real Talk, analyze themselves through simple Self Evaluation and become empowered to grow and change through intense Group Discussions.

So as you venture inside these pages, know that you are armed with a fresh relevant tool that will begin erasing, one at a time, the stereotypes placed on our youth and instead start equipping them with the knowledge to become better men and women for society.

How To Use This Book

There are countless ways to treasure the tools and lessons in this book. Let your ingenuity and creative ability be your guide to inspiring the youth within your reach.

Here are some helpful tips:

1. Investigate the brick (**Value**) for building good character.

2. Compare the **Opposing Principle** or habit and the results that follow it.

3. Identify the use of each value in someone else's life through real stories known as, **Real Talk**. Use this as the real-life example to show young readers that these values are reachable. (Note: Here's the time to get pictures and current facts involved in the study).

4. The reader answers a simple true and false **Self-Evaluation** designed to begin the process of growth. (This can be an open or closed exercise)

5. Finally, engage in insightful **Group Talk** discussions that empower each young person to internalize the values and critically think about its effect on their real life.

Thus, enjoy this book. Share it with your youth staff, use it to instruct your classes, use it as a reference wherever you are involved with youth and go forward building a better world one brick at a time.

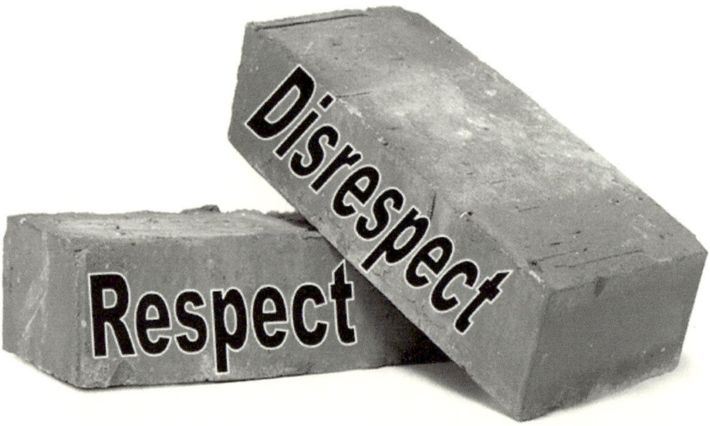
Respect
Disrespect

Respect

        I saw a poster that read, "You have to give respect in order to get it". That's on point. However, you first have to have an understanding of what respect is. To young people, giving someone their "props" is respect. That is, acknowledging that someone deserves honor, because they are handling themselves and their business acceptably. But the only way for you to begin acknowledging your satisfaction with someone else, to give them their "props", is to first be satisfied with yourself. You have to give yourself proper respect first. You see it's easy to feel good about someone else when you already feel good about yourself. It so happens that this is exactly where the disconnect lies for many young people when it comes to respecting the elderly, their country, their parents and their friends. If they have never been taught to have any

Respect / Disrespect

respect for themselves, then expecting them to respect others feels forced. And forcing them to respect others, respect rules and just about anything else only breeds rebellion. These rebellious feelings and the fact of inwardly feeling a lack of respect gives birth to what we know as, bullies. Bullies are simply kids, or sometimes kids who have now become adults, who don't feel respected and therefore tries to force others to respect them.

The whole foundation of respect first starts at home. There must be a structure in your home that models respect for you. Parents, guardians or adults in the home must lead by example in how to give respect. Before a young person forms any opinion of respect about the law, respecting teachers or other leaders in the community they must respect the authority at home. The way your parents talk to or about your teachers plays a major role in how you see them. And your view of someone or something shapes how you will talk to or address it. The way your parents talk about the president or police is the reference you will have that shapes your mind and how you see them as authorities. Young people can avoid a lot of scrapes with the law just by shadowing acceptable manners learned and views expressed at home, in their presence. The way many parents discuss religion or their views on other races will also have a direct influence on how a young person perceives them. Most importantly, the way the adults in the home talk to or show respect for their children will shape the way they ultimately view themselves. And how you view yourself will have the greatest influence on the way you see yourself in society. The foundation of respect in a good society is built on people who have good foundations of respect that where first built at home.

Disrespect

Let's start by pointing out what is not "disrespect". When a senior citizen is talking to you and refers to you as a boy/girl this is not disrespect. Think of it like this. The population of our elderly was born many years before you were even thought of, so to them you *are* a boy/girl no matter how old you become. So an elderly person addressing you in that manner should not be viewed as disrespect.

Let's say you've approached an attractive young lady and you are waiting on her to say "yes" to going out with you. She finally does respond but she says "no". Before you try to insult her by calling her out of her name or spreading lies about her because you feel disrespected, you have to know this is not disrespect. This is rejection. Both disrespect and rejection make you feel angry or disappointed but they are different. Think of it like this, anyone has a right to reject you (say *no* to you) but no one has the right to disrespect you. Rejection is one of those facts that must be accepted early in life because there will be many more experiences of it coming your way.

If a teacher in class tells you to shut up and sit your narrow behind down in the chair so you can learn something, don't take that as disrespect. Although your friends or peers are around and you might be embarrassed for being talked to like an out of control child, don't mistake correction for disrespect. Because of a teacher's responsibility to educate you and up to thirty others at the same time and to prepare you for a future you are not even sure you want yet, their correcting you becomes necessary to keep order. It's not disrespecting you because they have the position in the classroom, which gives them the authority to keep order in the best way possible in a given situation. Think of it like this, when a situation breaks out in a public place the police are called to bring order to that chaos. And because of their position it gives them the authority to keep that order in any way possible depending on the given situation, even to the point of using force. Just think of your teacher as the law in your classroom, take your medicine maturely and sit your behind down like you are told.

Respect / Disrespect

Lastly, if someone doesn't think you are attractive or you're not fly in the gear you're rocking, and they make it known to someone else or even to you, this is not disrespect. You're probably thinking, "yes it is!" Well it is not because the key to disrespect is it has to be forced upon its subject. You can't trip off everything someone else says or thinks about you. Everyone has a right to their own opinion, even your haters, and the Constitution of the United States of America gives them the freedom of speech to say so if they choose to. Nevertheless, just because they say it or think it doesn't make them right about it. They can't force what they think on you. Think of it like this. How can you feel forced by someone else saying or thinking you're busted when you already think and have told yourself you're fly? You left home that day feeling sure about that fact and no matter what anyone else said or thought about it, that fact would remain. And even if they expressed otherwise, there would still be no cause for retaliation. How many young people are dead today because they felt like someone else *having* an opinion about them was *forcing* their opinion onto them?

You can see what "disrespect" is not based on the examples given above. So what is disrespect? Disrespect is having and *forcefully* showing total disregard for others' feelings, property or

11

another person's well being. Usually this behavior is clearly demonstrated when someone is speaking extremely loudly about someone else in effort to get others to listen and join in. Also, mistreating another person in a bullying manner or threatening way in which they cannot or feel they cannot escape (forcing). This forcing is what breeds retaliation. In the present world we live in we are seeing too many young people go to an early grave because of the famous saying, "Ain't nobody goin' to disrespect me". The truth is that yes, there may come a time when someone will disrespect you probably because they don't respect themselves. Regardless if someone is using profanity or calling you out of your name, it's not a reason to start World War III. In reality it is not what people call you that matters, but it's what you answer to that does. It's time young people conclude that name calling and mouthing off is not enough reason to be sent to an early grave. And losing your life is not a worthy price to pay just because someone chose to disrespect you.

Respect / Disrespect

Respect

Real Talk

If the only standard for what respect is, is based upon experiences of being disrespected, how then can we expect change to take place? Many young people have never been taught or shown the right way to respect our country, the elderly, themselves, people in authority and so on. So we cannot justly become frustrated with their way of thinking. Making statements such as, "These kids today don't respect anything." or, "Why don't they just do better?" My question is, "How can they do better, if they don't know any better?"

Take Keisha for example. She is a very attractive student at 21st Century High. Lately, she has become seriously interested in dating. Keisha didn't grow up during the times when men pulled out chairs, opened car doors or referred to women as "Miss and Ma'am". Sure, she's been told that young men are supposed to have a certain level of respect for young ladies. She's been told they should talk to young women like ladies and be gentlemen toward them. The problem is, the only examples she has of what this looks like are how the men in her mom's life speak to her in a damaging way, or how her best friend is afraid of her boyfriend because he's always threatening her with violence. She is bombarded with examples of the opposite of respect.

One day, she was walking home past a group of guys that go to her school and they all turned their heads to look as she walked by. One guy said, "Ay girl." but she kept walking. Another called out, "Hey lil' mama." but she never turned around to feed into his foolishness. Then one dude, whose pants were sagging somewhere around his knees, became angered by her disregard. So, with his crotch in his hand, he yelled to his friends—loud enough for Keisha to hear, of course, "I know that trick don't think she better than us!" Keisha paused, thinking "Maybe I should just say what's up so they can shut up." but just before she does she recalls how she's always noticed Mr. Nettles who lives down the block speaking softly and sweetly to his wife *all* of the time. She remembers how he opens the car door for her. And how every week just before he carries the packages of grocery upstairs for her, he says "Hello, Miss." to Keisha, as she passes on her way to the corner store. Just then Keisha decides, "I'll just keep it moving because, these fools, they don't respect who I am anyway." and she walks on by.

Now if Keisha didn't have some sense of respect for herself she would have responded to this rude behavior out of ignorance. And even though she doesn't see it at home the small examples she does have are powerful enough to change her thinking and to inspire her to want something better for herself.

Food for Thought:

Believe it or not, there was a time when young men met a young lady's parents and asked politely for permission to court (date) their daughter before trying to holler at her. Maybe we could benefit by bringing some of that back. It would provide some needed accountability for our youth ending up right simply because they started out right.

Respect / Disrespect

Respect

Self-Evaluation

Circle one: True or False

True/False You fully respect yourself.

True/False I know how to give respect.

True/False To give respect is a personal choice.

True/False Respect is deserved not earned.

True/False I respect my country and its leadership.

True/False I can take respect from someone if they don't give it to me freely.

True/False All parents are worthy of respect.

True/False I know people in my community, church, and/or school whom I definitely respect.

True/False Being an adult makes a person automatically more respectful.

Respect / Disrespect

Respect

Group Talk

You're in line at a public restroom and it's your turn next. You've waited patiently, but an elderly person comes in and jumps you in line. What would you do?

You should only respect those in this world that respect you. Agree or Disagree.

When you are being bullied and you let it go on without end, you are showing respect. Agree or Disagree. Explain.

What would be your response to a person who practiced another religion other than your own in our society?

Are your parents respectful to people that have authority over them?

If you don't have respect for rules in our society, will it be possible to successfully work on a job that has rules?

When a boy/girl calls you out your name you should get even with them by fighting them. Agree or disagree? What should you do?

If you are a driving in a car and get pulled over by the police, how should you react?
      a. Talk to them like they are your friend.
      b. Get real afraid because you possibly will go to jail.
      c. Immediately answer all questions asked to you with "Yes, sir." and "No, sir."

Is it o.k. for an adult to disrespect a young person? In what ways could an adult be disrespectful to youth. How should you deal with that?

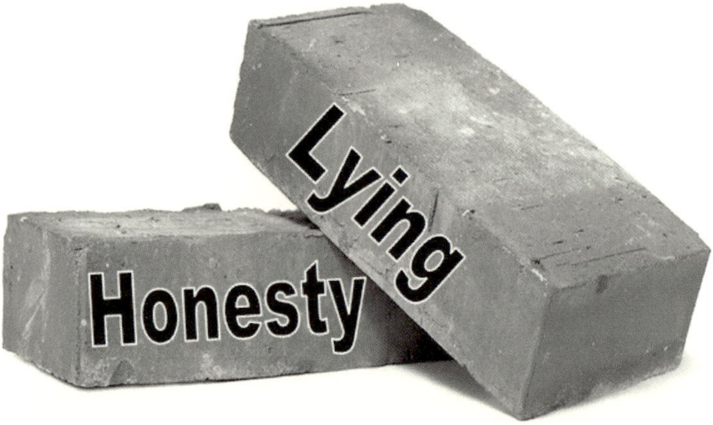
Lying
Honesty

Honesty

Doing what is right, for the right reason, to get the right result explains what honesty, also known as, integrity is. When you still do what is right even if no one was around to see you do what you do then you are an honest person with integrity. This value is what every good relationship in the world is founded upon. Whether it's a relationship between parent and child, friend and friend, girlfriend and boyfriend, employer and employee, honesty and integrity are the basis of a healthy bond. Whether or not you display honesty/integrity will be the measuring standard used to determine if you're a worthwhile person to do business with in the financial world. Banks will use the system of checking your credit report as a way to determine your level of honesty/integrity. It's true

Honesty / Lying

you can tell a lot about a person by what they do with their money. Of course, credit reports tell history of our spending habits, although it may not report a full picture of one's character. In reality, some of the biggest crooks in the world can have a perfect credit report, yet are of very low character. However, that doesn't eliminate the use of this standard. This standard exists because honesty/integrity builds trust between people. If someone feels you aren't an honest person and can't be trusted then any kind of dealings with you are off. You may not know it, but you are looking for honesty/integrity in your parents, friends, doctors, salesmen, teachers, churches and so on. If you've ever found an adult person to be lacking in their honesty/integrity you may recall yourself thinking or referring to them as a hypocrite.

Only honest people can really appreciate the importance of doing right for the right reason to get the right result. Employers terminate employees often because honesty/integrity isn't displayed. You may believe that this fact doesn't apply to you because you plan to use your slick ways to start your own business. Well, think of it like this, even if you owned your own business, customers would still need to know you as a person of honesty/integrity for your business to survive. To keep reliable employees who operate your business, your staff would have to believe your honesty/integrity will make sure they get paid at the end of a hard working week. Honesty/integrity is one of the most valuable traits a person can have and should never be taken for granted. Honesty/integrity should be taken seriously because once one gets a reputation for being dishonest or lacking in integrity it becomes very difficult, sometimes impossible, to change that view.

Honesty / Lying

Lying

      Lying operates on the snowball effect. Like a snowball that starts out small, but when it is rolled together it wraps more and more snow until it greatly increases in size. Once this happens, it is virtually impossible to unwrap the snowball and discover the place where the original size began. It works on momentum; the power to increase at an ever-growing rate. The purpose of lying is to cover up the truth. Yes, lying takes place when the truth is hidden altogether. Lying also occurs, when full disclosure is held back. This is what is meant by half-truths. Truth doesn't need any help. It doesn't need to lean partially on a lie to do its job. Truth is powerful even standing alone, so powerful that it can make a person free. Free of what?, a lifetime of guilt and shame.

Honesty / Lying

Nobody is a born liar, even though it may seem that way with some people. Children learn the power of language early on, usually around age 4 or 5. This is the age when they begin to want things and to test the boundaries set around them. Lying is one way of attempting to get what they want even when the boundary of NO has been set to prevent them from having it. Kids start using lying to get out of trouble, even though boundaries have been set to protect them. If these lies aren't stopped early this soon leads to more deception. This starts out very innocently, but this same child can end up very depraved. At its worst the person becomes a pathological liar (lying uncontrollably) about small and large things without any regard for the truth at all.

Why do people lie? People lie for many reasons; to get ahead, protect themselves from pain, increase financially or to be someone they are not. Parents can help young people to avoid the trouble brought on by lying through requiring them to come clean early in life. If you mess up then fess up. Tell the truth about it because it makes you a more trustworthy and guilt free person.

Liars are easy to spot. There are always behavioral clues present when you lie or when someone lies to you. Spot a liar pretty easily by noticing such behavior as avoiding eye contact, change of voice, fidgeting or shifty body language.

Honesty / Lying

A lot of "umms" and "ahhs" in an answer can also be a clue. Body language like covering face or mouth or constant fidgeting with your hands or legs can spell deception. Yet, the best way to detect lying is to listen for the contradiction in what a person says.

If you have developed a habit of lying, there is no perfect formula to stop it. It is best to deal with it before it is completely out of control. The only way to do this is to follow the Nike motto "Just Do It." It may be hard at first, but you will feel so much better and, in time, the people around you will feel comfortable in trusting you again.

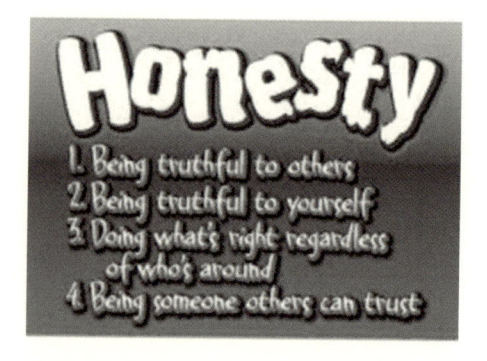

Honesty
1. Being truthful to others
2. Being truthful to yourself
3. Doing what's right regardless of who's around
4. Being someone others can trust

Honesty

Real Talk

George Washington, the first president of the United States of America, was about six years old when he like all youth made a discovery about being honest. He found an axe and like many curious boys started to play with it. He went around chopping at everything in his way. One day he came upon a cherry tree and he tried the axe out on it. He hacked the tree until it eventually died and fell over. A day or so later his dad noticed that the cherry tree was cut down. George's father was outraged and came into the house and demanded that someone tell him who had cut down the cherry tree. Just as the demand went out George came in with his axe. His dad asked, "George, do you know who cut down my cherry tree?" George could have blamed someone else because he was afraid but he chose to say, "I cannot tell a lie father, I cut down the cherry tree". His father was so proud of his son's display of honesty/integrity that he rewarded George generously.

This story of George Washington's honesty followed him from his youth all the way through to his leadership of this country. These are the kind of honest young people we aim to raise today who will lead in the future of our world.

Honesty / Lying

Honesty

Self Evaluation

Circle one: True or False

True/False   I don't see anything wrong with telling a little white lie.

True/False   I have never stolen money from anybody.

True/False   When I use the internet I always stay on good sites.

True/False   If given too much change at the store, I always give it back.

True/False   I never lied about being sick to miss work or school.

True/False   I have never done something in secret that I can't do in public.

True/False   When I know something is wrong I never do that thing.

True/False   When there is free candy out I never take more than my share.

True/False   I will never fake an accident just to get me money.

Honesty / Lying

Honesty

Group Talk

You are in a grocery store and to your surprise there is a fifty dollar bill that just fell from a woman's pursue. What should be done about this? Why?

How do we usually respond to people that are straightforward?

If you were in a classroom and the teacher walked out and said, "No one is to talk". Then the class bully talks and the teacher hears someone talking as she walks in, "Will you be the one to tell the teacher on the bully?"

People often rationalize their dishonesty by saying, "Everyone else is doing it so I will too". What do you think about this type of thinking?

If you could describe in your own words an honest person, what would they be like?

You find a cell phone and knowing you can go and get it changed over to your ownership, what should you do next?

Is there any risk in being honest? Is there any risk in being a liar? What are these risks?

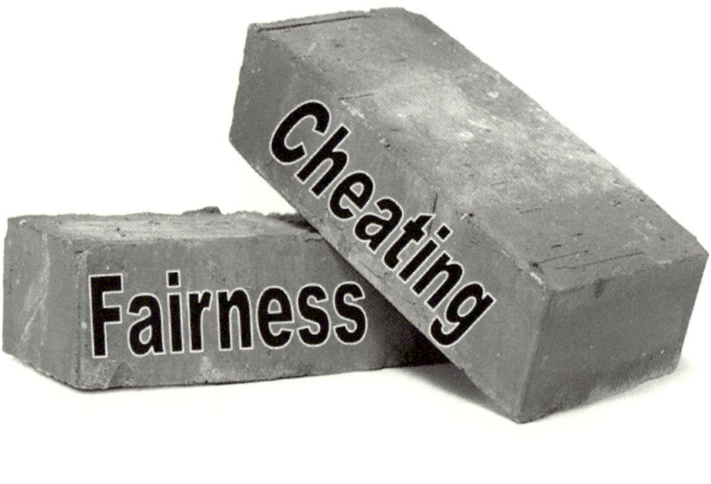
Cheating
Fairness

Fairness

We believe in being fair. But what is fairness? Is it all about people being totally equal? No. Fairness is not about being equal, because no two people are totally equal. Fairness does not mean everybody gets what they want. If this were true then our justice system would be perverted. Court cases would never be solved, laws would never be rewritten and this would leave our society ruined. We certainly can't apply fairness to appearances. If we could, that would mean that if something or someone looked good then it would only be fair that they *be* good. The same would be true for people or things that appeared to be bad. But we all know that just because something looks good or bad doesn't make it automatically so. There's always more than meets the eye when it comes to good and bad people. So what is fairness? Fairness is simply this, the act of treating someone in a way that is reasonably how you would want to be treated and not being judged without a good reason for being so.

There is a written and an unwritten rule that this country lives by. You've probably heard it called, "The Golden Rule." That is, "Do unto others as you would have them do unto you." Many parents teach their children to understand the idea that what goes around will, sooner or later, come back around to them. This idea is so embedded into our culture that when Americans are wronged we automatically shout foul play. Being fair is the one rule that was instilled in us as early as first grade, but somehow seems to leave us as early as middle school. We all learned it when the teacher said, "Play fair with one another, share your things with others and keep your hands and feet to yourself." These rules are set as the expectation of what we all *should* be doing. This is a good expectation, but we don't always see it carried out in reality. In a perfect world everyone would have an equal piece of the pie, but in this world people don't always treat you fairly just because you treat them fairly. This is the wedge that lies between the haves (those who seem to have it all) and the have-nots (those who seem to have nothing).

Nevertheless, our beloved Golden Rule is a

fundamental value that we should strive to live by. Thus the lesson to you is: treat everyone as you would want to be treated. And if for some reason you are not treated that way, remember the only person's behavior you can control is your own and just keep moving onward toward success.

Fairness / Cheating

Cheating

We live in a competitive world. We enjoy athletic competition, competitions with million dollar prizes, competitions for opportunities or just competition for the fun of it. Sadly though, this fierce competitive nature creates a world where the good guys sometimes finish last and this in large part, because of cheaters. There is a philosophy in all competition that celebrates the "survival of the fittest." This means the strongest, boldest, most fearless or toughest always wins. However, the fittest don't always play fair, sometimes they cheat to win. There is another common philosophy that says, "Do whatever it takes to win." It's a good philosophy yet cheaters also do whatever it takes to win. As you can see, cheaters use good philosophy for bad reasons.

So why do cheaters cheat—to win. And what's so great about winning? It usually comes with a reward. If there was no reward for the winner, people wouldn't be tempted to cheat. Cheaters are always desperate to win so they can get their hands on the prize, and they'll do it for just about anything. Think of it like this, if cheaters will break the rules in basic things like sports, academics, games, body building contests or even personal relationships then they will do the same in other more significant areas of life. At the very essence, cheaters are going to break the rules that are based on morality, ethics and goodness just to gain an advantage, just to win.

The problem is that cheating doesn't make winners it makes losers. When kids who cheat, get an A for work they didn't do, there is no motivation to work hard on the next task because there wasn't any hard work on their part in the beginning. They lose the personal responsibility to pull your own weight and carry your own load. Once you begin to cheat you lose the desire to be a real winner. The feeling of getting by or cheating and no one knowing it is what you start to really love. Then you'll find that once you're cheating so much it gets easier to do each time and harder to stop. Cheating becomes like a drug, the more you do it the more you've got to do it to keep up. Cheaters usually cheat as long as they don't get caught. You may be thinking, "That's the key, just don't get caught." But just like with using drugs, once you do it the more you want to do it. And

Fairness / Cheating

the more you do, makes it harder and harder to hide the fact that you are doing it.

So you want to win. There's nothing wrong with that. Winning is a great experience. No matter what we are doing, deep down we all want to be winners. But it's important to know what the real prize is. The prize is not the shiny token you get at the end of the contest. The prize is the inner victory of knowing that all of your hard work, your battling through struggles and overcoming your fears has taken you to the place you've been dreaming of. The journey is the real prize.

" I would prefer to fail with honor than to win by cheating."
Socrates

Champions pay the cost to win and that cost is never reduced nor does it go on sale. Young people must learn now that cheating robs them of that sense of accomplishment which comes from hard work. When you cheat, whether it's letting someone else do your assignment, taking pills or drugs to enhance your performance or copying your work from someone else—taking shortcuts, cheapens the success journey.

Fairness / Cheating

Fairness

Real Talk

Learn a valuable lesson from Glen. Glen cheated and lost his best friend and his girlfriend all because of some pretty unfair decisions. It started out very harmless, just a couple of funny comments on the computer. A contest was started on Facebook between Glen and a couple of guys to see who had the best stories to tell about boyfriends sneaking around on their girls. Glen didn't want to be found out so he used a different name and created a fake page to participate in the game. After a while, Glen got totally wrapped up in the hoopla. The stories eventually turned into lengthy tales with a lot of details about how Glen had cheated on his girlfriend with various other girls and when he was caught he did all sorts of macho things to put them down.

Then one day Glen's best friend, Jason, was pulled in on the conversation by clicking on a nickname just like his own and it linked him to the message board. While browsing the stories and laughing at the episodes being discussed, he stumbled upon some embarrassing stories that included very personal details, and were

Fairness / Cheating

also untrue. Of course Jason knew that no one but his best friend Glen knew him by that nickname. He wanted to confront him but because he was so shocked and angry he couldn't find words. He asked Glen's girlfriend if she knew anything about these stories which some of them included her name and pretty personal details about her also. She knew she and Glen were having a great relationship and simply dismissed the story as foolishness.

The next day at school, while she was standing at her locker a girl came up to her with a group of followers and began reading details from some of the stories being posted on the page. They all began making some insulting remarks about how her boyfriend was making a fool of her and everyone knew it. She was horrified. She went directly to Glen to confront him about this. He denied being involved at first. Later, his friend Jason confronted him and he joked about it saying it was all in fun. Well, Jason and Glen's girlfriend came together and demanded an explanation and Glen had no choice but to tell them the truth.

Seeing how immature Glen had behaved his girlfriend made up her mind that she did not want to date someone like him. She let him go but she struggled for the rest of the school year to clear her reputation of the things that had been said about her. As for Jason, he and Glen continued to play sports together but never said more than was necessary to each other. The damage had been done. Jason even lost his girlfriend in the process because she was never convinced that he was innocent of cheating on her. So, Glen found himself all alone and very disappointed. He kept telling himself how he should have stopped to think of how he would feel in the end and how it might destroy his friendship and relationship forever. He had no choice but to accept that even though he hadn't, cheating didn't pay. It was more trouble than what it was worth.

It sometimes takes losing everything of value to you before you understand the consequences of cheating. All cheating has some degree of an effect on you and those around you. If we would take a second in the beginning and imagine what the end will be like our decisions would certainly be fairer.

Fairness / Cheating

Fairness

Self-Evaluation

Circle One: True or False

True/False   I always treat people fairly.

True/False   Treat others as I want to be treated, is my motto.

True/False   If there are rules to follow I do my best to abide by them.

True/False   If my behavior is out of line, I consider the feelings of others.

True/False   I don't take advantage of people ever.

True/False   Being unfair to others is their problem, not mine.

True/False   Cheating is sometimes the easiest way around.

Fairness / Cheating

Fairness

Group Talk

What are the advantages of being a fair person?

What effect will cheating have on your character?

Former president Thomas Jefferson said, "If one asks for justice then justice is what one should get". What does this mean to you?

How should you treat people who are not fair to you?

Give an example of you being tempted to cheat, but not doing it.

Do you feel social classes that exist in our country like upper class, middle class and lower class are fair? Explain?

If being fair meant you had to give up something valuable to you to help someone else, would you do it? What are you willing to give up that is valuable to you in order to be fair to someone else?

Is it fair for your family to have tons of resources and not help a family with little?

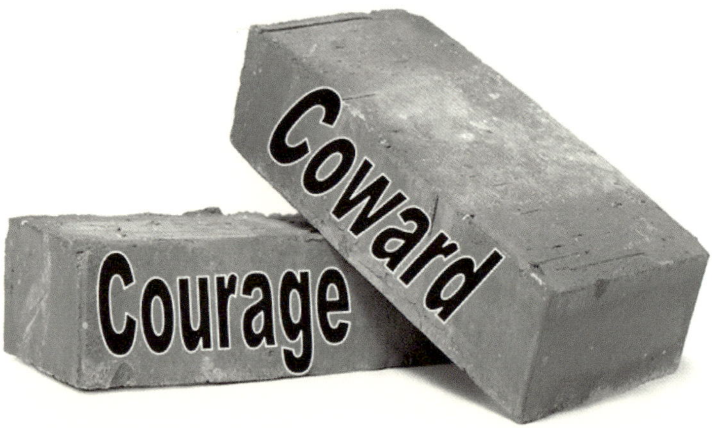
Coward
Courage

Courage

          This is a value that when used helps us to face the unexpected changes of life with bravery and confidence. There comes a point in everyone's life where you will either sink or swim, crash or fly. These experiences demand that we meet them with using some level of courage. Teachers and parents work overtime to inspire our youth to have the desire to step up to the plate in life. But to their dismay, fewer and fewer are coming up to the plate and even less are actually taking a swing at the ball. But the catch is, for you to have even the slightest chance of hitting a home run you must first step up to the plate. And if you really intend to get a home run you have to learn to swing for the fence. It will take courage to even begin to try this. In the great game of baseball, most home run hitters strike out much more than they hit home runs in a career. However, one thing is for sure, it takes courage every time to step up to the plate and it takes courage to take a swing at the ball.

Of course, this take-the-bull-by-the-horns approach is learned through a process. The first attempts are the hardest but courage means knowing it's hard but being willing to do it anyway. On one hand, we see it doesn't come naturally. On the other hand, there are three simple tools that can be used to help you move through this process toward having and using courage. You will find that if you use them regularly enough, courage will be so automatic for you that it will seem to come naturally.

Tool #1: begin watching and following other courageous people before you try it on your own.

This is an essential step in your success journey. You must seek out, read about or interview others that have climbed mountains you are about to climb. They can serve as guides to help you understand the journey you're on, answer questions when confusion or fear set in and even to cheer you on when you feel like giving up. Whatever situation you find yourself in, strengthen yourself through research of how others have used courage to face the exact thing you are going through.

Tool #2: before you can have courage you need to speak courageously.

This second tool is an extremely powerful tool which can work almost like a magic trick. Magicians don't actually have the power of magic, what they are great at is the power of illusion. They use the power of deceiving the mind or senses to believe that something *is* even though it may not actually *be*. When you speak courageously you begin to train your mind to believe what could be but may not actually be, YET. No one knows this better than a bully. A bully preys upon the timid simply by talking big. They create the illusion of toughness usually just because they are bigger. The key is, when you face people or problems that are bigger than you, not to fear. Someone or something being bigger than you doesn't make them better than you. Think of it like this, no one knows what you can really do, likely not even you do, but if you start talking it up with some courage that's half the battle and you might be surprised at what you can actually accomplish.

Courage / Coward

Lastly and probably most important of all is the third tool.

Tool #3: once you have courage—use it.

Many humans don't face challenges because they talk themselves out of success. It doesn't matter how much courage you have it means nothing if you never use it. To show you have a heart of courage you have to face some sort of challenge. And what's more is you have to do it now. If you're faced with a challenge and you know you have to deal with it you have to act on it before you talk yourself out of your own success. If you're not careful you will allow fearful and negative thinking to always outsmart your courageous thoughts. You have to believe you can achieve it and go for it with all you have.

Never forget that just like you can talk yourself out of success, you can take courage and talk yourself into success. Try using these tools today. Figure out where you're lacking courage and start by opening up your mouth and speaking things of success into existence.

Coward

Cowardly behavior shows up when you have a challenge that you know you must confront and you don't. There are many ways, good and bad, to confront conflict. The major goal is to confront it quickly and wisely to avoid becoming cowardly. A coward's behavior comes out in one of two ways. One way of being a coward is to do nothing about your challenge. The other way is actually the same as the bully we mentioned before—by doing some things that create an illusion of being tough when the reality is you are a scared person inside. Let's say someone you know is being bullied so much so that they think it is normal. This is definitely not normal and it is a horrible position for the person being bullied and for the bully to be in. In such a case both persons are being cowards.

Because of the challenges that surround growing up, all kids have the potential to become bullies or to be bullied. The constant name calling, nit picking, fault finding and teasing that go on all the time among youth can produce a generation of cowards. If this is not dealt with our young people are left alone to navigate through a jungle of fear and pressure. When youth don't have proper love at home, the feelings that surround this inadequacy come out as bullying. Then we have a misguided and scared child who is finding ways to attack others as a bully—a coward. What's worse is not handling this problem means there is a misguided scared child filled with insecurity who finds him/herself being a victim. And no one should be forced to be a victim.

These are 4 tips to help anyone escape the trap of cowardly behavior. **Tip #1: Make boundaries.** This means drawing a mental line in the dirt, so you will know how far you will go before you confront someone. **Tip #2: Say "No!"** If someone puts pressure on you and pushes you to participate in a way you don't feel comfortable doing, tell them "No!" Others will soon respect you for your assertiveness and it will likely keep others from trying you. **Tip #3: Use strong body language.** When you walk into a room (situation) don't be afraid to look people in the eye. Never let them see you sweat even if you are a little scared. Stand up straight and control any extra body fidgeting. Posture is important. The right kind sends a message that you are serious and should be taken seriously.

Tip # 4: Find a role model. Locate someone that has successfully overcome cowardly behavior. Use their example to help you deal with your challenge.

IMPORTANT NOTE: Take courage! If you are being bullied at school or anywhere else, find an adult in authority that will take immediate action to regulate the situation and put a stop to the bully.

Courage

Real Talk

      Nick Vujicic is a man that faces enormous odds everyday of his life with courage. He is a motivational speaker, a real estate investor, a writer, option trader and a community developer, just to name a few. Nick is unique because he was born having no arms or legs and to let him tell it he has no worries. Nick's mom was a nurse and she had been around hundreds of mothers and delivered hundreds of babies. Some of which were healthy and some were born with disabilities. She had seen it all until her own son was born limbless on December 4, 1982. There is no medical explanation for Nick's condition. He was just born like he is, limbless. In one of his talks he says that he is thankful that his parents or doctors didn't discover his condition while he was in the womb. He says because they might have encouraged abortion believing that his condition would not allow him to have any quality of life. Who knew the success that would be up ahead for Nick? From the start of his life limits was placed on him of what he couldn't do and what he couldn't become and what he couldn't have. He had to really use courage to go to school and be teased by other kids. He learned early that his only limitation was what existed in his mind.

Courage / Coward

Instead of concentrating on what he didn't have, Nick used courage to see what he did have and focusing on that gave him his reason for living. In a word, he is remarkable. He shows us that we all can be just as remarkable when we stop placing limits on ourselves. No one knew his future just as no one knows your future. When something is taken away from us and we still find ways to succeed in spite of human comforts, this type of behavior takes every ounce of courage we can find inside. Fear traps us and turns us into cowards but courage, when used, frees us and turns us into champions.

Pictures used courtesy of acidcow.com and myspace.com

Courage / Coward

Courage

Self Evaluation

Circle One: True or False

True/False   I stand up for what I believe even if I stand alone.

True/False   Just because someone is bigger than me I don't see them as being better than me.

True/False   Fear of failing doesn't stop me from trying new things.

True/False   When someone tells me I can't do something I simply stop.

True/False   I've bullied kids younger than me.

True/False   I know what it feels like to be bullied by someone.

True/False   I have courage but I don't know how to use it.

Courage

Group Talk

What kind of personal characteristics are required when facing new challenges?

Have you ever had to deal with a bully? Explain?

What stops people from taking a stance against things they know are wrong?

Does peer pressure have anything to do with how you dress, talk and think?

Do you think people are born with courage or it has to be developed? Explain?

What does it mean to have the courage to just be yourself?

What is your favorite movie that shows the characters displaying courage?

Name three things that is a difference between courage and cowardly behavior.

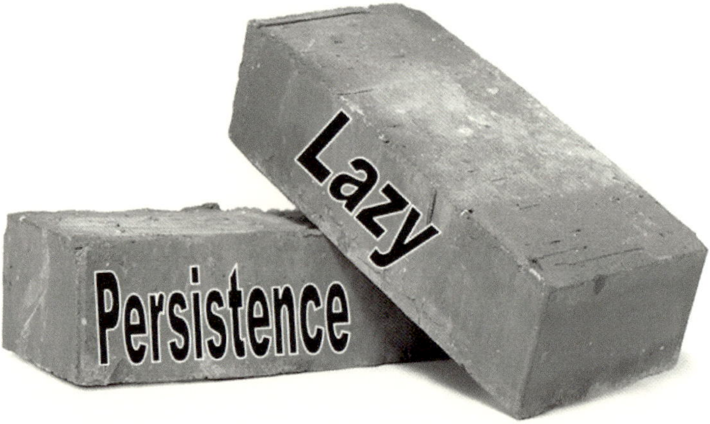
Lazy
Persistence

Persistence

        Insanity is defined when someone does the same thing over and over again expecting a different result. A drug user keeps getting high, all the time saying they'll quit the next time; this is insanity. It's insane because no matter how much the addict wants to quit, as long as they keep doing drugs they'll never quit.

        Persistence is a value that appears similar to insanity, but it is not the same. Yes, to be persistent you have to do the same thing over and over again but you're not expecting a different result you're expecting more and more of the same result. Persistence's reward is totally different because it is born out of a different purpose. Never giving up, staying on course, doing whatever it takes to keep moving forward, doing the same thing for a long time to get a little farther in the same direction are all expressions of persistence.

"If at first you don't succeed try, try again."

William Hickson

Hard work and sweat is the cornerstone of our American culture. A person's success is connected to how persistent they are willing to be. The secret to any success in any field of discipline is to never give up. As you are pursuing your life's dream you may fail 10,000 times over. Yet instead of saying you failed 10,000 times, change your perspective and say you tried 10,000 different ways. Michael Jordan said, "I've missed over 9,000 shots in my career. I have lost over 300 games, 26 times I've been trusted to make the game winning shot and missed, but because I failed, I persisted to succeed."

When we do fail, we must understand that failure is not final. People learn more about succeeding by getting it wrong than they ever do by getting it right. Picture a tiny drop of water beating on a concrete pavement over time. It's a small drop not making a great impact all at once, but with persistence it will eventually develop an indention in the hard surface. If it persists to drop over a long enough period of time, that indention will become a great hole. Persistence is powerful; this is how we got the Grand Canyon!

If you are going to ever get your breaks in this life, it is going to have to be led by persistence. This means, never taking *"No,"* for an answer, never being comfortable as the victim, and never giving up on your dreams.

Persistence / Lazy

Lazy

In the culture we live in, no one appreciates a user. It's unacceptable to get by on what someone else is doing for you when you can do for yourself; this is known as being lazy. Laziness is a force seen in the youth of yesterday, today and will be tomorrow. The reason laziness is so prevalent is because you will never convince everyone not to travel the easy route; but instead to practice hard work and persistence. As an athlete in my youth, I made a practice of never wanting the coaches to call me lazy. I always made sure I did more than my share to prove that I was hard-working and a dedicated player. When I grew older I carried that same work ethic into my adult life. I can sometimes even be a work-a-holic. So now I persist,in a structured way, to take at least one day out the week to relax. On this day nothing is done accept what must be done. The trash stays where it is, clothes where they lay and so on. This is a *planned* "lazy day." I know it doesn't seem natural to plan a day of laziness but by doing so, it gives me permission to take it easy without creating a bad habit of always being lazy.

Below are some behaviors that youth need to stay away from in order not to be considered lazy.
1. Playing the blame game
2. Sagging your pants
3. Cutting corners
4. Lack of foresight

The Blame Game: In a lazy person's world the blame game works like this, "My mom didn't take me to get it so I just don't have it." "I can't do my work because I didn't have enough time after I watched eight hours of T.V. last night." "The reason I can't get a job is because "The Man" won't give me a chance." Excuses, excuses! They are horrible traps into laziness. Even if you are not a lazy person, overall, excuses have a way of making you appear to be. Trade the excuses in for responsibility through being persistent. The persistent response would be to ask, "What can I do differently to make me more successful at this point?"

Sagging: Sagging is a lazy fad that most respectful people hope goes away really soon. But since it is here, it must be said that it sends the resounding message, "I'm lazy." All of our youth has heard, "No one is going to hire you coming into an interview with your pants hanging off your butt." Well, it just makes sense that if you straighten up for an interview, to straighten up for good. The problem is, too many youth find this realism amusing mainly because they don't understand the fundamental concept of not being too lazy to work. Sagging your pants creates the impression that you are aimless, undetermined and unconcerned about how you're seen by others. No decent company is interested in investing time and money into a person with this outlook. This trend truly reflects on the job that parents are not doing at home. No self respecting parent would let their child leave the house with their pants hanging off their butt. And even if you don't agree with this then just know that this is the exact conversation the self-respecting parents are having about you. Non-lazy people do not sag their pants, at least not intentionally.

Cutting Corners: There is an age-old illusion that there is a fast way to reach success. Everyone has to resist the temptation to believe this myth and it begins while you are in your youth. Cutting corners allows lazy people to cheat, steal and lie for advancement. They are under the false impression that this will make the job easier. It actually creates more work when you miss details the first time and have to go back and correct them later. Non-lazy people make a practice of making every effort to go above and beyond the normal to reach their goals.

No foresight: Foresight is having the ability to think ahead, having vision. When you have a lack of foresight it means you usually have no thought of or plans for the future. In order for lazy people to develop some foresight (vision) they must begin immediately working toward a change. If this isn't done they'll soon find they can't see past unemployment, freeloading, not having any education and just low quality of life in general. Non-lazy people know people and plans perish because of the lack of vision. They practice persistence by first writing it down and then working with complete conviction until they see they vision realized.

Persistence

Real Talk

Colonel Harlan Sanders had only a pressure cooker in his hand and a secret recipe in his heart of southern fried chicken. He believed he had something special but received over 300 rejections of his dream before he found someone to believe in him. He rejected the rejection over 300 times; now there are over 11,000 KFC restaurants in 80 countries around the world.

Rick Little, at 19 years of age, wanted to start a program that would help kids in school learn strong communication and life skills. He wrote over 155 foundations asking for help but received no reply. To make ends meet he had to start sleeping in the back of his car with mostly peanut butter and crackers as his only meal. He never gave up his dream and eventually, the Kellogg Foundation gave him $130,000 to fund his dream. Rick and his team now have obtained over $100 million dollars to further the Quest program helping 3 million kids, in over 30,000 schools nationwide; all this because a 19 year old guy rejected rejection and stayed persistent in following his dreams.

It would do you good to learn now that rejection rides along on the journey to success right beside persistence. Just one great opportunity could make the multimillion dollar difference out of countless rejections. Keep trying. When you come to a road block take a detour but don't quit. We give up too easily when family and friends don't support what we are doing. To every "NO" you need to start saying, "NEXT." If you keep pressing toward your goal, your "NEXT" will soon outweigh every "NO" that you've ever heard and your story of persistence will inspire many generations of young people.

Persistence / Lazy

Persistence

Self Evaluation

Circle One: True or False

True/False   I take rejection well. I always say "Next." to every no.

True/False   I always finish what I start.

True/False   I keep a positive outlook. When things don't work out I try to see the big picture and learn from my mess ups.

True/False   I'm disciplined enough to go hard in some areas but not all.

True/False   When others don't believe in me, I change my plans to something more acceptable.

True/False   I've set some goals that I have not gotten to yet.

True/False   I'm not lazy at all.

Persistence

Group Talk

Do you think it is by chance that successful people become successful?

When you try hard and you don't make it, you accept that it's your fault?

How many times have you tried to start something and it didn't work? Why?

Name four things that cause people to give up and quit?

Honestly, how do you rate your practice of persistence on a scale of 1 to 10? (1 lowest; 10 highest)

Why is being lazy so popular among youth today?

Have you ever blamed another person for your lack of accomplishing something?

Does sagging make you appear being lazy or persistent?

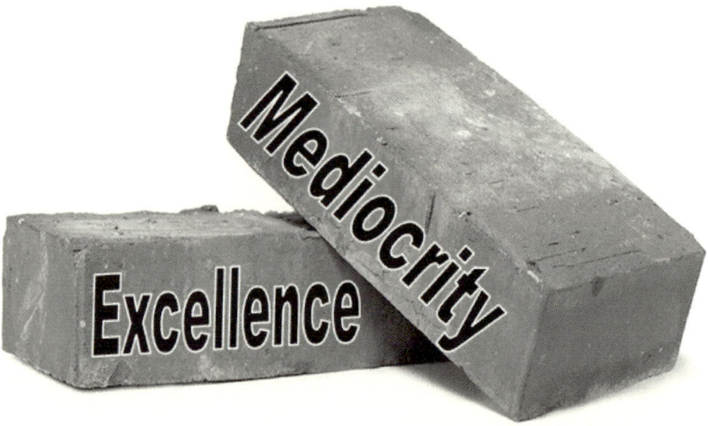
Mediocrity
Excellence

Excellence / Mediocrity

Excellence

The heights of great men reached and kept didn't come by sudden flight but they while their companions slept were toiling upward through the night.
Henry Wadsworth Longfellow

There is an unseen standard that is set at a high level, which great achievers strive to reach and surpass. This is known as the mark of excellence. Never doubt that you can achieve whatever you believe, but know there is a risk of sacrifice involved. You must put that little extra effort in all you do if you plan to be extraordinary. If your competition runs two miles a day, you need to make a practice of running three. If your competition is writing four books a year, you need to be sure to write five. If your competition gets up at six a.m., you have to be up at five a.m. to maintain your edge. When you learn this value early in life, you will certainly go farther than any of your less dedicated companions.

The simple question that you need to ask yourself in your quest for excellence is, "How bad do I want it?" An "A" student hates making anything lower than an "A". Everyone knows making a "C" is average and is also a passing grade; but if an "A" student receives a "C" they are completely dissatisfied. They may even flip out in their demand for an explanation or give up just about anything to make a better grade. They have developed an appetite for excellence and they can't stomach anything else.

Make the choice at this stage in your life to surround yourself with people who are going somewhere. Why should you settle for less when there is so much more in store for your life? Young ladies, "Why settle for a zero, of a man, when you can have a hero?" Young men, "Why settle for a chicken-head, of a woman, when you can have a queen?" There can be no comparisons made when you expose yourself to excellence. The value of excellence can be seen in something as simple as how one walks, how they keep their lawn, how they turn in their homework or how they treat other people. When you want excellence for yourself you want everything and everyone around you to be excellent as well. Older adults have a couple of true sayings that illustrate this concept. First, "Birds of a feather flock together." Second, "If you lie down with dogs, you will get up with fleas." It is true that if you build relationships now with people who also value excellence, they can serve as a power team to help support you in securing your future.

Excellence / Mediocrity

Mediocrity

Mediocrity is an uncommon sounding word that's all too common among our younger generation. Sadly this is the highest level of achievement that some people learn to reach from their youth. Mediocrity, doing just enough to get by, can be found in schools, on jobs, in raising a family and much more. What's worse is when a person of great potential dies with their only accomplishment being that they were average. No flair, no special thing about them, no important contribution to society. It's heartbreaking to imagine that this is the category in which most of our world fits. If you survey to find out what people expect in this society it is so far from average. Who wants an average career, to go out to eat at an average restaurant, to go on an average vacation—no one. No one strives for mediocrity but not striving will almost guarantee that you'll get it.

America holds excellence in the highest regard. America's pass-time, baseball, has filled its major league teams with the best of the best players. The same is true for the NBA and NFL; they're overflowing with nothing but the best. You won't find any mediocre athletics being sought out and drafted.

We are doing our future generations an injustice to allow them to only settle for what is average. "So, what do we do to remedy this tragedy?" The answer is exposure. We must expose our young to excellence. If the only things youth from lower income neighborhoods are exposed to is welfare, food stamps, violence, unhealthy single-parented homes, low education standards and improper sexual values then this is all they will ever desire. If the only things youth from upper income brackets are exposed to is being serviced and pampered, taking advantage of the poor to get ahead, selfishness and greed then that's the only thing they'll ever desire. Yet if you take these same kids-of-promise and show them a more excellent way of life they would surely desire that over the latter. If the only option placed in front of a hungry child is poisoned meat, since this child doesn't know any better he will eat it and then die. But if you place healthy options in front of him or the knowledge

Excellence / Mediocrity

of how to get his own food, he will choose to live. Technology, mentor programs and internships place these options at the fingertips of all youth. These should be made available to as many youth possible; for in them, they can find a vehicle to go anywhere and experience things that exposes their interest to excellence. Then and only then will settling for less cease to be an option.

Excellence

Real Talk

When excellence is practiced it is presented in humans going above and beyond the call of duty. Walmart advertises that they have the lowest prices guaranteed. They are willing to match any competitor's prices to keep your business. How can you beat a store like that? This kind of going above and beyond the call of duty, is what landed Walmart as the number one retail store in the world. Being excellent is not an option it's the standard.

Terry Fox just kept saying, "Just one more telephone pole." Having lost his leg to cancer in 1980, Terry Fox, made the choice to run a Marathon of Hope across Canada to raise money for cancer research. 24 miles a day is what he ran with an artificial leg! He ran 143 days like that before his doctors discovered that he had lung cancer. He died a few months later, but his story of reaching for excellence inspired thousands of people. Today the annual marathon ran across Canada is named the Terry Fox Run in his honor and has raised $340 million for cancer research, so far. Before Terry died, he

Excellence / Mediocrity

was asked how he kept going even when he was exhausted, he said, "I just ran to the next telephone pole." Think of your journey like that, just one more pole and you can make it! Regardless of the odds, regardless of the struggle, regardless of the road ahead you have to keep running for just one more pole.

Excellence

Self Evaluation

Circle One: True or False

True/False   I am ready right now to take my life to the next level.

True/False   I feel I'm on the verge of something great.

True/False   I take constructive critiques on what I do well.

True/False   I am guilty of doing just enough to get by.

True/False   Being excellent is too much work.

Excellence

Group Talk

Do you think it is important in developing your character to practice excellence?

Have you started surrounding yourself with a power team of excellent people? Explain?

Are you settling for whatever comes your way? How or how not?

Do you require the best of the best even if it offends others?

Is your attitude based on how high you can go?

What happens to the human drive when there is no greatness to strive for?

Is it important to you to make A's in your school subjects?

What does determination mean? Give an example

Finish this statement:
To put excellence to work in my life, I will have to ….

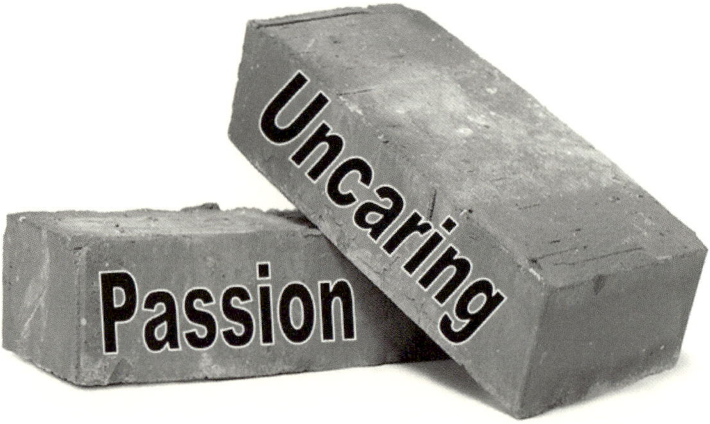
Uncaring
Passion

Passion

This value called passion has fueled all successful people to live their dreams to the fullest. Life's struggles can take a lot from you and out of you, but you can't allow it take your passion for living your dreams. Passion, though often mistaken to be related with sexual involvement, it is not the same when relating it to living your dreams. Here, passion is the desire that fuels you to do whatever you truly want to. Passion is going after what you really want to get. And whatever your particular truest desire becomes known as your—you guessed it, passion. It is that thing you have been thinking about all the time, dreaming about and can't seem to go to sleep at night until you talk about at least a hundred times to somebody.

Many people don't do what they want to do in life because they haven't figured out what they are passionate about. How do you know what that is? The way to find what you are passionate about is by asking yourself this one question, "What is that one thing, above all else, that I really want to do for the rest of my life? As a young person, ask yourself, "Am I headed towards doing what I really love in life?" If your answer is "no." then it's time to stop and start again. You don't want to end up working for the next 30 years doing something you don't love to do. The most successful people I know love what they do so much that they would do it for free if they had to. Yet, they followed their passion and they have found a way to make a living doing what they truly love to do.

If you always visualize yourself doing something else other than what you are currently doing, then you need to *do* something else than what you are currently doing. Start preparing your life for your dreams. If that means you have to educate yourself more to do what you really love to do, then do it. If it means working part time in the field of your dreams or volunteering to be around the area of your passion, then do it.

To identify your passion means to understand that there is something that only you were born to do. You have accepted that and now you can't stop pressing until you find it. Put everything on the line to fulfill it. If it is a noble and worthy goal that will give your life meaning and purpose then it is worth giving it all you've got. Some people are born to be a teacher; some, to be a preacher. Some a singer, a writer or whatever it is that brings them contentment and fulfills that burden of carrying around an unlived passion. What were you born to do? What is your passion?

Uncaring

You can see that there is a strong power of influence among all youth. Youth inspire other youth to join clubs and athletic teams, listen to certain music, wear certain fashions, go to church and the list goes on and on. Unfortunately, there is just as strong a power of being uncaring at work in our communities. The behaviors that point to this in our youth are easy to see. Those that have stopped caring, tend to shout profanity at anyone, including parents, in a way that everyone can hear them. Their pants are usually sagging off their behinds so the whole world can see that he or she just doesn't care. Piercings and tattoos are permanently attached all over their bodies in plain sight without concern for their professional or personal impressions. Young girls are showing how they don't care by showing everything including their "birthday suits" (bodies) to get attention from boys that don't care either. The overwhelming behaviors that show little to no respect for our elderly population who has come on before us come from uncaring young people. If you dared to ask any of the above mentioned, people about their actions they would probably say, "I don't care. I'm going to do me." Passion has been replaced with this cold-hearted, uncaring feeling for life.

People who don't care about themselves can't be expected to care about anybody else, adults and youth alike. And as a result, crime rates will be high, drugs and gang banging will be present in our community because of the fact that somebody stopped caring. Trash will stay in the alleys, pit-bulls will remain the usual pet on the loose, housing will continue to be mediocre and drop-out rates will keep getting higher; all because somebody stopped caring. This is why an elderly person can tell a decent kid to stay away from "those kids" because "those kids" and their behaviors are of low character and hanging around them can bring you low.

This must be stopped. One sure-fire way to do that is, if you want to be a caring and successful person start hanging out with caring and successful people. Until you are strong enough in

Passion / Uncaring

your character to not be influenced by people who just don't care, you should avoid them. Uncaring people are toxic to your health, your future and dulls the brightness of your passion for life.

Passion

Real Talk

Tony Dungy grew up in a home where his parents instilled values in him from the beginning. He was taught at an early age to handle problems without yelling but with wisdom and a cool head. He was an outstanding athlete in Jackson, Mississippi, where he went to high school. Talented enough to go to the next level, he played at Minnesota University for four years solid. He was drafted to play defensive back for the Steelers. During his short time there as a Steeler, his team succeeded at winning a super bowl championship. After his playing days were over, Tony had several coaching jobs. Later, he became the head coach of the Tampa Bay Bucs. While coaching the Bucs, Tony took the team to the playoffs often, but never to the big game (Super Bowl). Because of this fact, the owners of the Bucs fired Tony Dungy and his entire coaching staff. After the termination he knew he could get another job in the NFL, but he didn't know when. He received a call from the Colts offering him the head coaching job there and it was a good fit. The Colts made the playoffs every year, but, like the Bucs, never to the big game. Finally, after many years of hard work, much humiliation and many losses, in

Passion / Uncaring

2007 Tony Dungy won the Super Bowl. This was a professional and a personal victory because that year he became the first black head coach in NFL history, to do so.

Tony Dungy is a great football player and coach, but his real success is in his character. He is a man of faith, one who leads his family and who mentors youth. He is a compassionate giving man that is passionate about high morals and doing the right thing with integrity. He has since, written a best -selling book, as well as many other books on leadership, coaching and just being a complete person with God's help. He followed his passion to the top.

Passion

Self Evaluation

Circle One: True or False

True/False I'm already doing what I'm passionate about.

True/False I don't know what I'm passionate about.

True/False I will be satisfied just being around the area of my passion.

True/False I'm not worried about it, I have plenty time to focus on my passion later.

True/False I can live without what I'm doing right now.

True/False I talk about my area of passion every day.

True/False Nothing is more important to me than accomplishing my passion.

True/False Being focused on your passion makes you a selfish person.

True/False If I start focusing on my passion at this age, I'll miss out on the fun things in life.

Passion / Uncaring

Passion

Group Talk

Name the one subject you could talk about for hours and hours.

Do any of the things you love to do involve working with other people?

What are the thoughts that occupy your mind, which you can't seem to let go of?

Write three things that you have done in life that has given you the most fulfillment.

Pretend you have reached the end of your life and you look back. What is the one thing you've done or you became that was most beneficial?

List five people, you know, who are passionate about something, but they are doing something other than that.

Do you care about your community, school and family enough to make a difference? Explain

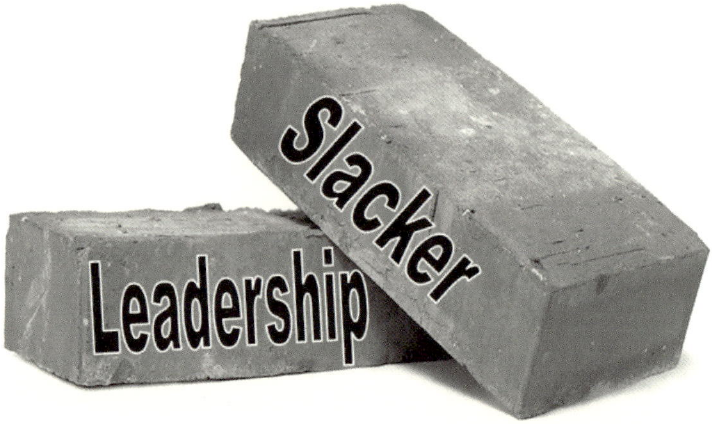
Slacker
Leadership

Leadership

Leadership is a skill and inner value that helps us with direction. It answers the question, "Where do we go from here?" Everyone is going to have to develop the leader within. We all are placed in areas where somebody is looking for leadership. Whether it is on the girls' volleyball team or at the scene of a house on fire, leadership must kick in. The objective here is to help you mirror some traits of good leadership. If others are going to follow you, you must honestly ask yourself if you would follow you and why. If you were in a crowd and had to choose a leader from among them, would you choose yourself as somebody worthy to follow? Leaders are proven by the people that follow them. The traits below are a few proven qualities that all leaders need to prove they are of good character.

Leadership / Slacker

Leaders must...
   *Take worthy risks
   *Be honest,
   *Have vision,
   *Be competent.

Taking risks is a part of the daring side all of us have. The quote says, "There were two paths in the woods, I decided to take the one less traveled. " Who is to say that the road less travel is right or wrong? You will never know unless you take a leap of faith and try.
Everybody plays it safe, but leaders figure out what's worth losing for, move to the edge of take the risk. They are the people who we admire for walking down paths that seem impossible.

Be honest with people who are looking to you for help. Followers know leaders make mistakes, but they also are waiting to see if you will be honest enough to admit your mistakes. Being a leader doesn't mean being perfect because being a leader is possible for any human but being perfect is not possible for any.

Leaders have vision. To get yourself, family and others who are depending on you to the next level from where you are, it is going to take vision. Looking ahead with the foresight to having something better and preparing for the future is a sure trait that all good leaders have.

Being competent means you following through with *how* you plan to accomplish whatever it is you desire to do. Many will expect you to be competent because of your leading position, yet you will have some to whom you must prove your ability. These are the people who will follow you once they have seen some signs of success and they see some of what you've led them to believe, come to past. Remember that a large part of being a good leader means getting the job done.

Slacker

This trait is what you see in people that have something to say about what everyone else is doing, but are also the same ones who refuse to lift one finger to do anything worthwhile. **Slacker** is a term that became popular during World War I. It described those who avoided war efforts to help keep America safe and free. Anyone that dodged the military draft was known as a slacker. In the American culture, a slacker is usually someone that has a history of not valuing citizenship. This is because citizenship requires everyone to do his or her share of work to preserve this country.

When leaders are pushing the people forward slackers are there to pull people back. When goals are to be accomplished with a group effort the slackers are always right there with their selfish pulling force. Slackers cause businesses to close, football teams to lose, families to stay non-productive and the country's freedom to be threatened. The slacker has the mind-set that, "I'll do it later, maybe even tomorrow." This thinking is the direct opposite of a leader who thinks, "Why put off for tomorrow what can be done today." A sure way to be a failure is to procrastinate, by dodging personal responsibilities.

The goals you set for your life should be approached with some urgency. Do it today! Don't wait! Life's goals might even be given an expiration date like a carton of milk. You buy some milk and it has a certain date to drink it or it will spoil. The same is true with being successful; though it is not as final. Right now is always the time to begin, no matter how young or old you are. We should give ourselves a small window to get the lead out of our rear ends and get to the finish line. Slacking will most certainly see to it that you never make it there.

Leadership

Real Talk

There are people who will disagree with everything you decide to do when you serve as a leader of anything. These people have no dreams and they don't want you to have any either. If you can get past people's rejection of your ideas, you will make it as a leader. Monty Roberts did just that. He is the author of **The Man Who Listens to Horses**. When Monty was in high school he was asked to write a paper about what he wanted to do when he grew up. Monty wrote that he wanted a 200 acre ranch to raise Thoroughbred racehorses. The teacher received the paper, graded it, and gave it back to him with an "F" for his grade.

The teacher explained that his dream must be more realistic. Monty had the vision is took to be a leader. Monty gave the teacher the paper back, and said, "You keep this F, I'm going to keep my dream." Many people think if they can't see your dream for you that you can't see it for yourself. Who would think that a boy living on the back of a pick-up truck in a camper would be able to get enough money to fund his dream? How can he do it and have funds to pay ranch hands and other expenses? Well, Monty did it because leaders stick to their dreams even if they are the only ones sticking to it. Monty now owns a 154 acre ranch in Solvang, California where he trains thoroughbred racehorses and trainers too. I'm sure that Monty, at times while riding, must think about what his life would be like if he had simply followed other people's opinion of what his life would be. True leaders hear the doubt, face the critics, and know the risks involved but they lead anyway.

Leadership / Slacker

Leadership
Self Evaluation
Circle One: True or False

True/False I have the ability to lead others.

True/False I use my influence with my peers to lead them to do what's right.

True/False I away plan for the future.

True/False If everyone is doing something wrong it don't have an effect on me doing it too.

True/False When I fail I bounce back quickly.

True/False When I mess up I confess my wrongs.

True/False I like to hide in the back, so I don't have to be seen.

True/False Leading people is easy for me.

True/False I'm accountable for my own actions.

True/False Areas where I need help leading others I watch other who are successful at doing it.

Leadership

Group Talk

If Kate jumped off the bridge would you jump also?

Do you have an emergency plan made up at your home if things go wrong? Explain?

When I receive feedback that is not positive about my behavior I work on it right away?

What are three main areas you will have to be a leader in, in life? Why?

How do you use your time wisely to manage your day to day schedule?

Do you think it is important to study other leaders that have been successful at what you are doing?

Name 3 leaders that you model yourself after?

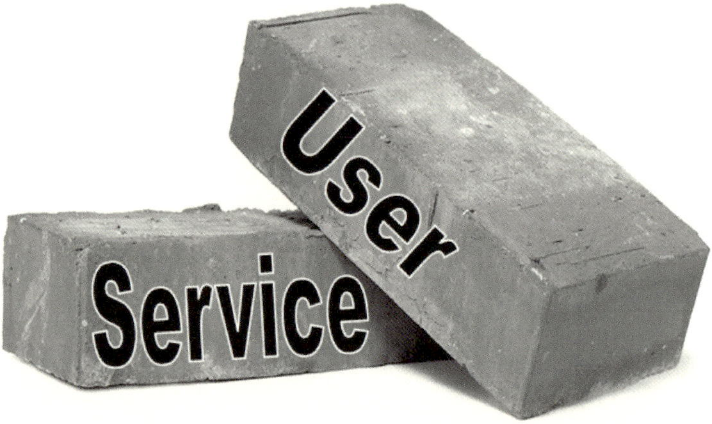
User
Service

Service

"The greatest among you are the servants"

Service is simply work done for someone else. Sometimes this is done for payment, but many times it's done for free. In service of the community, the country and our religious services we all find a sense of belonging. You find out, a lot about yourself when you lose yourself doing for other people. Most people that understand the value of service do so because they want to bring about a change in this world. The best way to change the world is to become the change you seek. For young people this has to be learned early in life. If you want to see hunger ended, then get busy serving the hungry in this area. Whatever the area you're concerned about, the best way to help change it is through finding a way to serve in it. The good thing is that you don't have to go all over the world to be of service, just start in your city. Is there a local park in your city or maybe even several that can use some upkeep? Is there a community living facility for the elderly near-by? Are there allies with trash dumpsters and cans overflowing in your city? Is there a local soup kitchen or clothing shelter? Just start answering these questions and many more will follow. This could keep you busy in service to others for the rest of your life.

The way to greatness is not through how much money you have in the bank, having the fastest cars or the largest house; it's through having a heart to serve. The world couldn't function properly if we didn't have people with a heart to be of service for the causes they are passionate about. Youth must know that you can get things a lot sooner by not sitting around waiting for someone to give them to you. Rather, plan today to give of yourself to truly get a great return in life because of your service.

Being dedicated to being of service to others has an amazing effect of making you feel like a better person. The greatest opposition to people being service minded is the problem of being selfish. Selfishness keeps you focused only on yourself. You don't make time for others because you are so focused on yourself. Selfish people not only focus only on themselves they also want everyone else to focus only on them. But usually what happens is when you're only focused on yourself, others will have no interest in making you a priority. The key to turning this around is service. If you make it a personal priority you'll find that in return for you being available and willing to serve others they will happily serve you.

Service / User

User

This behavior is so easy to pick up, but so hard to put down. Users suck people, places and things dry of all life. I had the privilege to coach men and women struggling with drug addiction in Louisiana. I noticed that the same behavior of using drugs is the same behavior present when using people. Users use just because that's the thing to do at that time. These individuals of low morality are always looking for a chance to get over, trick somebody out of some money, hustle you on the next big thing and so forth. I do believe that there is hope for the user if they want to make a change for the better. Users are people and people are subject to fall, but they can get back up again. We don't usually call people that drive cars, car users or people that ride horses, horse users. Yet the behavior of one taking advantage of another human can only be described as a people user. As long as there are kind-hearted people in this world, there will always be users as well. The kind-hearted are the ones whom users prey on, taking their kindness for blindness. Listed below are four tips you can use to stop being taken advantage of by users.

Notice patterns If you are the one always doing the listening, always lending the money, always being available then this is a pattern for being used. Usually your time and/or money is what users are after. They will come with a certain look or tone of voice that seems sincere, but it's just another scam.

Say "No" People that end up being taken advantage of by a user usually suffer from what is known as, the *disease to please*. This person wants everyone to like him/her and continually accepts others demands on their time, resources and energy. While all this is going on, you are being drained of your personal power. Begin now by practicing saying "No" to them. Stand firm without giving in to their undesired requests and avoid being ripped off.

Make them wait You need to become very unavailable all of a sudden. If the user is not using you they will go find someone who they feel can be used. People are creatures of habit. If they can't get

Service / User

it one way they will try another, automatically. Don't answer your phone, don't go to visit them, become like a ghost to them and see the difference it will make in your peace of mind.

Ask for proof The most effective way to help someone that you have reservations about is for them to provide proof to you of what they want. Ask questions. "What are you going to do with my tools or money if I give it to you? What plan do you have to give this back to me? Have you tried anything or anybody else?" If the explanation they give is not up to your liking don't proceed. Proof holds them accountable and secures your given assets.

Remember it's your choice whether to help them or not.

Service

Real Talk

The most successful countries, communities, churches, businesses or schools are the ones that put people first. People are the most valuable investment of any; period. Without people you would not have anything. Keeping service to people as the top priority will produce better results for whatever business or relationships you have. The Ritz Carlton hotel is one of the many people- driven businesses. They begin each day with what is known as "line up". This is where they get to talk about experiences with customers, resolve any problems and discuss ways to improve service to people. At this time they are able to tell the "wow" stories. With every story told all of the employees feel inspired to do more work and provide better service for people.

Here is one story in particular, shared in Jack Canfield's **Success Principles:** about the Ritz Carlton, Bali. There was a family that came to the hotel as customers and this family had

Service / User

brought along specialized milk and eggs for their son who suffered from food allergies. Upon arrival, the parents noticed that the specialized eggs and milk were damaged. The eggs were cracked and the milk was soured. The Ritz manager and staff immediately went to work and searched the town, but couldn't find any appropriate items. There was an executive chef that remembered there was a store that sold those kinds of items in Singapore. He contacted his mother-in- law in Singapore, asked could she buy the products and fly to Bali with them. Well, she did and all of this extra effort went a long way with the family. What family wouldn't want to stay at a hotel like that?

Service / User

Service

Self-Evaluation

Circle One: True or False

True/False I do what needs to be done in my community.

True/False I love being served by others.

True/False It makes me feel good to do community service.

True/False I check on elderly people at least once a week.

True/False Community service is overrated.

True/False I volunteer on a regular basis.

True/False I don't care what happens to others as long as I'm ok.

True/False The only way I would do community service is under the obligation of the law.

Service / User

Service

Group Talk

Do you think serving other cultures can improve the way you view them?

Have you ever organized a community event to raise funds for a good cause? Explain?

Have you volunteered at a non-profit group before?

Why is it important to help out with blood drives?

Can you and a few of your friend organize a new comers group to welcome new neighbors to the community?

Do you have the talent to make food baskets for seniors in nursing homes?

Do you feel it is important to adopt a street and keep it clean of trash? If yes, how would you organize this?

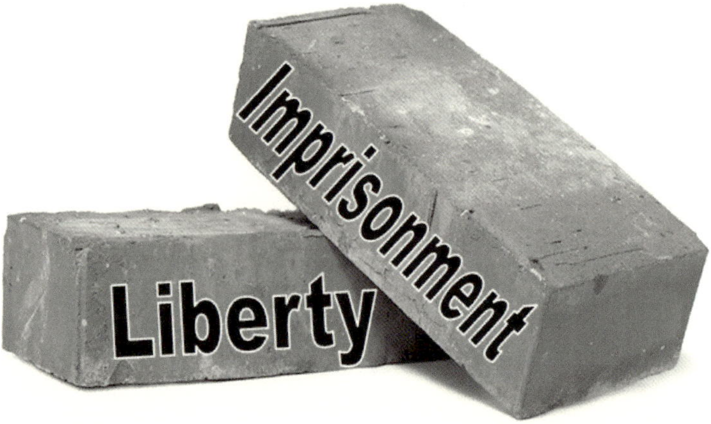
Imprisonment
Liberty

Liberty / Imprisonment

Liberty

This character value is one of many cornerstone truths that this country was built on. True liberty may not be practiced by all, but it is available to all here in America. The First Amendment to the Constitution of the United States of America is among our greatest of the amendments. It guarantees America's citizens freedom (liberty) of speech without censorship. Upon that first freedom rests all others that we share in this country. The value of liberty is protected by our constitution because it is the single greatest value at stake in this world. All of the wars that have been fought have been directly or indirectly connected to the protection of our liberty. This is why our youth need to know that freedom isn't free. Many different people that make up America, all have contributed to the fight for and protection of our liberty on the world's stage. Somebody must go to war, shed blood and many times die to keep our liberty secure.

Freedom isn't free; it comes with a healthy price to be paid. Freedom is not just special in this country, but liberty is of the utmost importance around the world. People of good character that have experienced freedom want everyone else to experience freedom also. When you believe all men are created equal, you also want to believe all men have the right to be free. The only reason another human would attempt to enslave another human is because they don't view the other human as an equal part of humanity. When someone views you as less than a human they will treat you any kind of way. We must act responsible with our freedoms so others will value it also. What is the point of living if you can't have some kind of freedom? This is why people who are passionate about freedom live with this affirmation, "Give me liberty or give me death."

Imprisonment

When one doesn't act responsible about the freedom they have imprisonment is the result. The most common thought of imprisonment is when one goes to jail. However in America, jail is not total imprisonment, but it is an extremely limited function of your liberty. In jail is where many prisoners gain a whole different view of freedom. One that is irresponsible about their liberty usually gains respect for it after it is taken away. Youth that want to live the "gangster life" have the least amount of value for their own liberty. They give their freedom away to a group or leader who imprisons their thoughts and dictates their actions. Since they live in

Liberty / Imprisonment

imprisonment with no value for their liberty, then they have no appreciation for other's either. They manipulate and attempt to threaten and force other young people to respect their barbaric way of life and when they choose not to, they ignore your liberty and try to harm or kill you. These lowly people usually spend their whole life imprisoned in selling drugs and engulfed in crime then ultimately end up behind bars with almost no freedom or dead with absolutely no freedom.

But going to a physical jail is not where imprisonment begins, for many it is what it results in. Truthfully, by the time a youth reaches jail you will discover this person lived in imprisonment long before they got there. Imprisonment, at its worst, is not when someone else locks you away from your liberty but when you lock yourself away from fulfilling your own dreams and your freedom to really live life. If young people are not taught good character lessons and disciplined for unfavorable behavior early on, it's likely they will spend a long life imprisoned in negativity, unproductiveness, in jail or worse, dead. Stopping youth from being imprisoned must start with healthy patterns of success at home.

The following, are some sure examples that will almost always lead our youth to a life of imprisonment. Teens having babies is one sure way to lead our youth to imprisonment. Teens are still kids themselves, and most are not even capable of caring for themselves. Thus putting them in an instant parenting position can lead to raising a dysfunctional child. Kids have no earthly idea on how to raise another kid; it takes responsible parents to do so. And when a young person becomes a parent, way too soon, it can take away their liberty to live their life to the fullest. Concerned parents must make the effort to stay all up in their teen's life in order to ensure that they are not involved in sexual relationships that will contribute to the sky-rocketing statistics of teen pregnancy.

A parent never requiring any success at educational standards is a road leading to imprisonment. When a child's behavior or grades become negative at school, and a parent doesn't get involved to help the school help their child, no one else will. If the child brings F's home on their report card, early prevention must be put in place to correct the shortcoming. Finding tutors or after school programs to get the child back on track is a parent's job in order to help their child. More than anything, demanding a level of excellence in education and not tolerating anything less will prevent a child from being imprisoned in a life of low achievement.

Overwhelming dislike for authority exists in children that talk back to parents, ignore teacher's advice, disrespect elderly members of society and claim they hate the police. These young

Liberty / Imprisonment

people usually have a problem with authority. These behaviors going unaddressed are almost guaranteed to lead a young person to a life of imprisonment. Without these behaviors being stopped early, these youth will likely end up in jail, where they won't be able to enjoy any of their liberty.

Liberty / Imprisonment

Liberty

Real Talk

Henry "Box" Brown was born into American slavery. At the age of 15 he was made to work in a tobacco factory in Richmond, Virginia. While working at the tobacco factory he met and married another slave. They had three children together, but one day the worst thing in Henry Brown's world happened. The slave owners of Henry and his family decided to make a profit by selling Henry's wife and kids off to another slave owner. Henry could do nothing to stop this transaction and felt powerless as a father and husband. He made a vow to never have such a horrible thing ever happen to him again. This is where his thirst for freedom and appreciation for liberty began. It was established because of the pain he endured.

Henry Brown devised a plan to mail himself to a free state. He paid $86 out of a life's savings for his package to be mailed. James McKim, an abolitionist, would receive the package (box) once it reached Philadelphia. Henry was boxed up and then shipped. While being mailed, his "box" traveled on ferry boats, trains and wagons. Being handled by hands that laid him upside down for many

Liberty / Imprisonment

hours, he remained in that box for a total of 27 hours. He finally made it to James McKim where they broke open the box and heard Henry "Box" Brown say, "How do you do gentlemen?" Liberty has a price and Henry "Box" Brown paid the price and risked capture to be free. Henry never went back south again and he goes down in history as the first and only slave to be shipped to freedom in a box. He became a speaker against slavery and would tell his story many times over, about how he was shipped to freedom in a box. Is your liberty worth risking your life for?

Liberty

Self-Evaluation

Circle One: True or False

True/False I know what the meaning of freedom for me is.

True/False I feel bad to hear about other countries that don't have liberty like I have.

True/False I use my freedoms under the law to the fullest.

True/False I have had times where I didn't want my freedom.

True/False I know the history behind American songs of freedom.

True/False I understand how being involved in a gang can mean giving up my liberty.

True/False The only form of imprisonment is being locked up in jail.

True/False Having a baby at a young age still gives a person all the freedom they could want.

Liberty / Imprisonment

Liberty
Group Talk

Do you think that your freedom is the most important value you have?

You are free to eat any kind of food. How would you handle a person that said they only ate vegetables? Explain?

Can you identify any decisions you have made or experiences you've endured that have threatened your liberty?

What are some of the ways you have exercised or abused your freedom of speech this week?

Name four things all free societies have in common? After naming these things, explain your listing?

What would our country look like if we never protected our freedom?

Why is it important to celebrate the armed forces that protect our freedom?

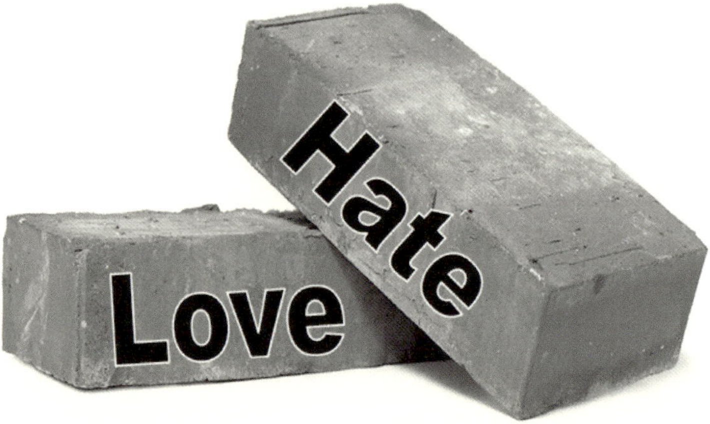
Hate
Love

Love

The strongest of all emotions and values is love. This character value identifies one who seeks the best good for someone else's best interest. There are several examples around us where love is being expressed. During the Christmas season, you can find Americans in the spirit of love who seek out others that may have less, in order to share with them. We see love expressed when someone chooses their favorite charity to give to or to serve for. On the surface this is what love looks like, but it is not the essence of what love is. For I'm convinced that one can give without loving, but one cannot love without giving. Someone could stop on the street and give terrorists money because they are out asking for money to bomb a group of people and not love what they are doing. Yet on the other hand, nearly no one could pass up someone in need and say, "I love you" and never give their time or resources to help that person.

General compassion for others and their situations is at the heart of love. Others' pain and struggles bring out the best good in us to help. It is very selfish for you to have all the gold and not be willing to share it with your fellow neighbor when there is a need. All the non- profit organizations that are in operation in the world is based on a basic love for humanity. Regardless of the profession, one must appear to be compassionate about people to have the power to inspire other people to follow their leadership. The saying, "People don't care how much you know until you show how much you care," is true today and will be true as long as humans exist. Love is what makes the real difference in our world. When you give love, love is given back to you in some kind of way. The greatest institutions in our country are built because of the value of love. Hospitals, orphanages, churches, food banks, shelters, clinics all have a common desire to see society better. We will never have a great society until people show great love for one another.

Hate

It is true that it takes more facial muscles to frown than to smile. The same truth applies to hate and love. People must work overtime, around the clock, to hate another human being. This behavior is characteristic of the dark side of human nature. Hate is a learned behavior usually passed on by generations of thoughtless ancestors. People find it easier to hate than to just tolerate others' differences. Fear of not knowing about a race or religion compels some to hate. Effort must be taken on the part of every human to mutually understand and accept other's differences. Hateful people are usually lazy and shallow in their effort to get to know others outside of themselves.

Hate is such a repulsive behavior in a good and

Love / Hate

decent society that laws had to be created to govern it. You will not find laws prohibiting how much you can love because history shows this is good for the world. Yet hate can become so dark that it leads to criminal behavior.

Haters miss out on a wealth of relationships with some fabulous people. Relationships with the human family is one of the greatest things you can have. Today, young people say things like, "Don't hate on me because I look good." This is a lesser form of the meaning of hate but it comes from the same mentality. Haters are people that like to put others down or to set traps for others to fall in. Wouldn't the world be a better place without people who think and act with hate? Although you think you would be better without these types of people, if you change the way you look at it you might realize that you probably wouldn't be. Look at haters this way, they give you free advertisement. Because they are always talking about you to someone else, it doesn't matter if it is good or bad, the advertisement is good for you. The more haters talk about you it only lifts you higher. So instead of wasting energy on wishing your haters would go away or returning the hate in an effort to overpower them, accept their dislike for you as motivation to keep doing you. Thus, view your haters as elevators to lift you to where you really want to be in life.

Love

Real Talk

One day Keke overheard her parents talking about her little brother's health condition. The parents were at the point that they didn't know what to do about their son's illness. They started crying and talking back to one another out of desperation. The mama said, "We don't have the money for that costly surgery, it is going to take a miracle." Keke heard this and figured in her mind that she could somehow get this miracle for her little brother. She ran up to her room, reached for her coin jar which was full of coins and dumped them out onto the bed. She said, "This will buy my little brother that miracle he needs so he can get better." She got a paper bag filled it with the coins, ran to the nearest pharmacy. When she arrived in the pharmacy line she was exhausted. There was a man in front of her who seemed to be taking longer than expected with the person at the pharmacy counter. Keke was through waiting and pulled the man's coat. He turned to her and said, "May I help you little girl?" "Yes", she replied "I'm here to buy my little brother a miracle." The man replied, "I'm not selling miracles nor do I know where you can buy one. Why do you want to buy your little brother a miracle?" "He is real ill and my mama said it's going to take a miracle to fix it." He asked, "How much money did you bring for buying this

Love / Hate

miracle?" "I brought all of my coins." she said. Little did Keke know that the stranger in line was Dr. Jurith Wellington, a well known, surgeon. Dr. Wellington took the little girls coins and her hand and said, "Lead me to your brother." The doctor was so moved because of the love Keke had for her little brother that he performed the surgery at no charge to the family and the illness of her little brother was gone for good. After the surgery the parents thanked the doctor, but told them, "Don't thank me, thank Keke for the love she had for another human life."

Love

Self Evaluation

Circle One: True or False

True/False   I love myself.

True/False   I was taught how to love at an early age.

True/False   Love for other people is easy for me to do.

True/False   When I see people different than me, I decide not to put an effort to know them.

True/False   Compassion is in my heart but not in my actions.

True/False   When people hate me I have trouble loving them.

True/False   I practice loving others as I love myself.

Love / Hate

Love

Group Talk

Why do people carry out hate crimes against people of different religions, cultures, sexual orientation or gender?

If my friends don't love a person of a different culture I usually join in? Explain?

List 3 acts of compassion that you can do for another person to show love for humanity.

How do you know that what you call love is really love?

Can one love someone else without giving things needed to fill their voids?

If all of the evil people in the world were the only ones available to be loved could you do it? Why or Why not?

Does love from the heart or from copying a learned habit?

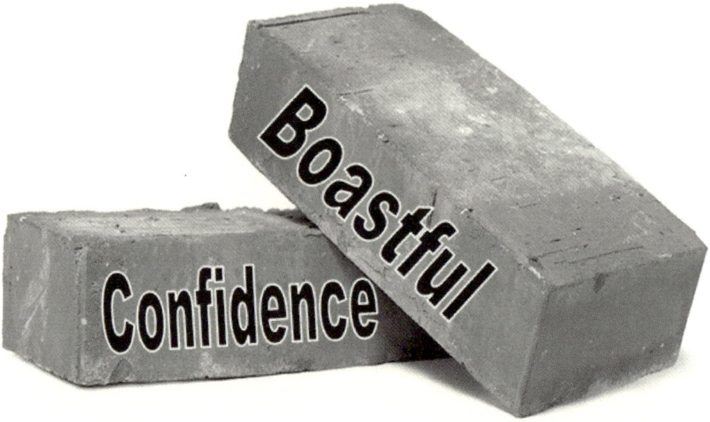
Boastful
Confidence

Confidence

This character value is not automatic it is learned from an early age. Whether you see yourself in a positive or negative light was influenced by your home-life and social environment. Your belief in your abilities were developed the same way. But, how you look at yourself today is not necessarily how you will look at yourself a year from now. Your confidence level will shift as you get older, sometimes back and forth with each year. The older you get the less you usually care about what people think of what you are and what you believe. You gain more solid ideas of what you think about who you are and what you believe. And your confidence level is fueled by your own thoughts more and more.

Image is of key importance to strengthen one's confidence. The objective of this section is to help young people build their confidence. The success of accomplishing this will have far

Confidence / Boastful

reaching effects on their futures. No one will hire an insecure, timid young adult who's looking for a job. Employers can tell when someone fills out an application or comes in to be interviewed for a job, where the confidence level rests.

Here are some major things our youth need to know about confidence. Use these tools to improve and present yourself in the most confident way possible.

1. When talking to someone, you need to have already thought through what you want to say then speak. Lose the "uhm's" and have answers for the "I don't know" questions before even being asked.

2. Non verbal language must be strong as well. If you walk into a potential job opening and you are asked to have a seat, the employer will be determining by the way you walk to and the way you sit down in your seat, if you're confident about the interview.

3. When reaching out to shake a hand, firm handshakes are remembered far longer than soft ones, for men and women.

4. Look someone directly into their eyes when they are talking to you and when you are talking to them, this says you can be trusted.

5. Limit extra body fidgeting and playing with your clothes because that says you're nervous.

6. Remember you're been watched from the time you walk in to the time you leave, so act as if you're already hired until you get hired.

Confidence first begins in the mind. Start the day off by telling yourself, "I can do this", and watch everything line up with that confidence. The power of thoughts work both ways—positively and negatively. If you start off with that inner voice of doubt saying that you can't do it then normally you won't. Confidence is key and developing it is a must.

Boastful

This behavior works in opposition to our confidence. Confidence is power under control, while boastfulness is power out of control. We are not usually comfortable around boastful people. The topic of a boastful person is almost always her/himself. Who wants to be around another human that has nothing else to talk about except them? Labels like "big headed" "arrogant" "conceited" or, "vain" are given to this type of people. You can be pretty sure when someone has to talk very highly of her/himself they are compensating for something they lack or fear that they lack. When you have to tell someone over and over how great you are it is not to convince other people, but in attempt to convince yourself. And when you're not sure of yourself you drain others' ability and desire to tolerate your presence. These people don't usually have many friends or perhaps, they have too many friends but none that they can truly call a friend. We can liken this type of person to a volcano that bursts with hot lava and ruins everything in its path. Boastful people ruin relationships with others because there is too much self praise and not enough mutual appreciation.

Sometimes it can be confusing on whether or not someone is boastful or if they're just confident. The two are confused a lot in our modern society. What's the difference? We cheer for this type of attitude when a football player of our favorite team is running a touchdown and stops before the end zone and starts dancing or for the baseball player who hits a homerun late in the game to give the home team the edge, then turns flips rounding third base. We cheer on this type of boasting in sports, but we surely don't want to see it in church leaders, presidents, community leaders or teachers. Being boastful is different from being confident, don't confuse the two. Boastful people think too highly of themselves and too little of fellow humans. Whereas, confident people think very highly of themselves and yet are humble enough to surround themselves with other people whom they see as being even more highly.

However small or large the role a person or situation may play in our society, humility is the way to greatness. Being confident in your own talents and/or accomplishments is wonderful. It is especially valuable to having strong character. Having this character trait works at its best when you don't have to boast and beat your chest, just to do you.

Confidence / Boastful

Confidence

Real Talk

Calley was an overweight kid from the time he entered preschool. He found comfort in food. He would eat when he was angry, when he was happy and sad. Whatever emotion he experienced he would find comfort in putting food into his mouth. This went on for his whole childhood into his early adult years. Calley said, "Going to school was the worst part of my childhood because kids were so cruel to me." Kids would tease him by shouting fat jokes to each other in his presence and name calling directly to his face. One kid brought a pillow to school, stuffed it under his shirt and said to the other kids, "Hey look at me, I'm fat Calley."

Calley hated walking in front of mirrors. He saw himself slipping further and further into hiding each year. But, in his early 20's he notice a Nike poster that said, "Just do it." For the first time in Calley's whole life bells went off in his head and he decided that day he would lose the weight—forever. It was very difficult to get started at first. He kept at it for the next several years while starting and stopping. He never gave up on trying and hearing the three words "Just do it." Calley committed himself to the process. Soon others started noticing his weight loss and that became more fuel for him to keep going. He was determined to get his confidence back. Calley said that his drive to lose the weight came faster when he realized he could die from his obese state. He said, "I'm going to live to exercise all day or die and be dead all day." Calley lost the weight and his confidence went through the roof. He started dating which he thought he never would do, and found the confidence he needed to open a gym where he motivates others in his past condition to "Just do it."

Confidence / Boastful

Confidence

Self Evaluation

Circle One: True or False

True/False I lack personal confidence.

True/False The strongest area of my character is confidence.

True/False When I'm in front of people I'm at my best.

True/False When I pick places to sit in a classroom I always sit up front.

True/False I face the day with a smile even when I know it is going to be a hard day.

True/False I say to myself I can do anything I put my mind to.

True/False I have no clue what it feels like to be criticized by others.

True/False When I'm around certain people I find myself acting differently than normal.

Confidence

Group Talk

Is there a certain style of clothes that make you feel confident about who you are?

If you had more confidence in an area what would you do more of?

Have you learned what your insecurities are in your character? If so, explain?

Could you stand up in front of a crowded room and sing even if others didn't think you had the talent to do so?

Is there an educational goal you haven't meet yet that is keeping you from being your best self?

Would those around you say you are confident, boastful or insecure?

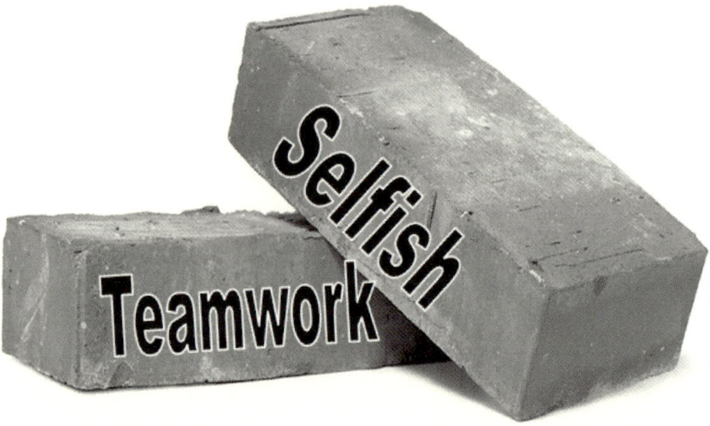
Selfish
Teamwork

Teamwork

One of the greatest challenges to anyone that has ever started anything is getting people to work together. People can be very inconsistent and very selfish when faced with the value of teamwork. If there is one thing Americans learn early in life it's self reliance. From the time we start walking, all through school and into the work place self-reliance is encouraged. Thus this is not bad, but it presents challenges to the fabric of teamwork. But it is important for you to learn now that no one can succeed alone or live in this world alone. We are all interconnected.

Youth that play sports or get involved in group activities early in their development have a very good chance of displaying the character trait of teamwork. Whether you are good at

Teamwork / Selfish

it or not, working together is the way our world operates. "None of us" is as good as "all of us," is the belief that pulls people to work together. One great way youth can become engaged in teamwork is to give them something exciting to figure out together. Placing them in a position where they can't call their own shots and be their own boss, but have to rely on the group to progress forward. This type of experience brings out everyone's character as a team-player or not. Just think of the television show, "Survivor." Some people you love because they strive to succeed by using the strengths of their team and others you despise because they'll do anything including sacrifice their teammates for their own benefit. If you rather it the other way around, it's time to check your own character and value for teamwork.

When teamwork is the objective, we want our character to row in the same direction as the team. For those who are out-going, teamwork is easy, but for the rest of us that like to be private and independent, we must be forced out of our shell to work with others.

There was a group of porcupines that wandered out of their nest on a winter night. The porcupines began to get cold that night and they all start moving close to one another in attempt to get warm. Their moving close together caused the porcupines to get stuck to each other. Therefore, some of the porcupines that didn't want to put up with the pokes went off that night and slept alone, while a small group of others endured the pokes and slept close together that night. In the morning someone came by and saw the small group of porcupines still alive because they had slept together though it hurt to do so. To their surprise, the ones that choose to be comfortable and slept alone froze to death in the cold of the night. Teamwork is important even if you don't like some of your fellow team mates, or if it's uncomfortable to be around them. But you should work hard to develop your understanding that each member of the team and each experience can be used for the survival of the whole.

Teamwork / Selfish

Selfishness

There is certainly nothing wrong with being an individual. All of us are very unique and no two people are alike even if they happen to be identical twins. There is a purpose carved out just for you and only you can accomplish it in this world. But being an individual does not give us permission to be selfish.

Selfishness is a formed behavior that starts as a baby. Every time the baby cries here comes mommy to see what the matter is. As this continues the baby begins to believe: 'whenever I want attention I can just put on a weepy show and they'll come running.' They get used to people saying how pretty they are and showering them with all this attention and to a kid, that has no other references of how to process all of this, selfishness is just around the corner. Now this is not to say babies don't need to be showered with attention. They actually *do* need to be early in life so they can establish feelings of self worth and confidence. Have you ever noticed how little ones don't hold back when they get a chance to shine? They don't even know what it feels like to be insecure yet and this is a healthy part of their development. However, there is a point where this desire for attention must be put into perspective or it will breed a mighty selfish person. Measures must be put in place to ward off selfishness. When babies reach crawling stage and they play with other kids on the floor, the toys become the objects of attention, so toys must be shared to help fight selfishness. Tough love helps fight selfishness; saying no to a toddler, child and teenager is necessary to set boundaries. Parents must set times when youth can socialize, surf the net, come home for the evening so they understand that there are other elements and people to consider in how you use your time.

It helps to know that young people, children, have a subjective (me-first) view of the world. They don't always see how what they want, think and do affects other people. This is something they must be taught. School is a great place to learn a sense of social skills and cooperation. Church is another wonderful place to practice these skills but it all begins at home. Young people develop the skills at home first, that will teach them not to display selfishness, to play fair and to be considerate of others' needs. In these small but valuable lessons character is born and shaped into what kind of human this one will be.

Teamwork

Real Talk

The miracle of stairway B is a heroic story of teamwork. The first responders of that tragic day in American history were NYFD fire fighters. The planes hit the North Tower first and then another hit the South Tower. For those that were to escape both towers, they had to use an emergency effort of teamwork. Everyone that was in the towers had only one safe way out and that was through the stairways. The elevators weren't working so many that couldn't get to the stairways had no way out. Many had to burn in the fire and some even chose, tragically, to jump. This was a day that will forever be remembered by those who were there and by the world who was watching.

Teamwork kicked in to evacuate the buildings. One could only go as fast or as slow as the person in front of them. No one was thinking about who had more money, who lived in the biggest house, what color this one was or who was better or worst. There was one goal: survival and that would only be reached through teamwork.

Teamwork / Selfish

There was a fire company going up a North Tower stairway, Stairway B, while Josephine Harris, an employee was coming down. She was so tired she could not go on and the firemen decided to help her down out of the tower. That decision to think of someone outside of themselves is what contributed to the saving of their lives. Everyone that didn't get out the North tower before it collapsed was killed, including over three hundred brave fire fighters. However, inside the center of stairway B, fourteen people were working together, and a miracle happened. Suddenly, the North Tower collapsed while these people were in it with tons of debris and dead bodies all over the place. After hours of attempting to locate any live person and finding none, radio contact was finally regained by the fire and rescue workers. They radioed for anyone who could hear their voices to signal if they were alive. To their surprise and in the midst of so much death and tragedy, a sunbeam was able to light a way for the firemen to identify the location of the people trapped in Stairway B. They were rescued, and the crew says it was only because everyone chose to work together to be saved or no one would have been saved at all.

What a wonderful example of teamwork!

Teamwork

Self Evaluation

Circle One: True or False

True/False I like working by myself.

True/False I never look for help. When I run into problems, I figure them out on my own.

True/False Me, myself and I is the only team I need.

True/False I pick up the momentum if whatever group I'm in slacks off.

True/False Crowds make me feel comfortable.

True/False I work well with people I don't usually like.

Teamwork

Group Talk

Give an example of you successfully working together with a group. What was your role? What was the project?

In your opinion what makes teamwork work?

Have you been a part of a team or group that failed and it wasn't because of you? What happened? How did it affect you? Have you been a part of a team or group that failed because of you?

Should you be the one that a team or group designates to be in charge?

What personal traits do you have that cause you to fit in with others?

What are three character flaws you can improve on to be a better part of the group?

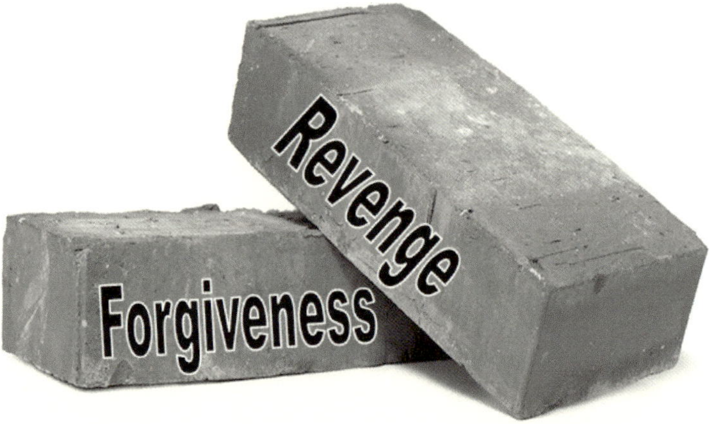
Revenge
Forgiveness

Forgiveness

This character value is special to all humans everywhere because for all the flaws in others and in ourselves, this value is there to cover them. Simple interaction within the human family will have occurrences of conflicts and offenses arise. The mistake many make is to take up a feeling of resentment when these things do happen. For example, someone may have hit you in the face in front of the whole 2nd grade class and caused you to become extremely angry. But, now you are in your early 30's still walking around angry at everyone and all of the relationships you have are being harmed by your unresolved anger. Forgiveness gives you the power to let it go.

Forgiveness / Revenge

Forgiveness is releasing the resentment you have against someone; to not hold a grudge. Forgiveness is the ultimate gift that, when given, has the amazing power to give back to you. You see, if you forgive someone who has done wrong against you, it releases them from error but it also releases you from anger and resentment; it frees you. In life, painful things will happen and there is no way around it. When they do, you have two choices: you can use the pain as a prison or a pusher. To those that hold grudges this pain becomes their prison, only to cause them to be unhappy and miserable for the rest of their life. To those who choose to forgive, this pain becomes the pusher that propels them further into their own happiness and freedom. Restoration of relationships that have been ruined comes through forgiveness. You have the opportunity to start now, as a youth, using this valuable tool. This tool works two ways because when you are a person that is willing to forgive others are likely to forgive you. Keep in mind, the same way the wrong and hurtful things that have you so angry and seeking revenge against the person who did them to you, could have someone else out there right now angry and seeking revenge upon you because you have done something unknowingly wrong and hurtful to them. Now is the time to consider forgiveness; if not for any other reason than to free yourself from the situation and the anger you have toward them.

When you really forgive it is not with words only, it is with actions as well. As the saying goes, when deeds speak words are meaningless. To really forgive another person, you must treat that person like they have never wronged you before. That's true forgiveness. Many people are not at this level of personal growth, but getting to this level and being able to forgive makes you a better person for humanity.

Revenge

When anger in someone goes unresolved for too long, resentment sets in. Once resentment sets in and stays too long, it takes on the form of wanting to get even, wanting revenge. Revenge or vengeance is a very dangerous and powerful emotion. Two wrongs never make a right, it only breeds more vengeance. Revenge has crippled and killed many young men. Many young men are in the grave this day because they wanted to prove to someone else, "I ain't no punk", and then chose to seek revenge which ended in killing someone. Furthermore, it is not just young men seeking revenge; girls seek it just as much. When girls get into fights they may try to damage the opposing girl's face, for life, by scratching or cutting her. But it must be made clear that nothing can be solved or gained by more revenge being taken out on one another until one feels they've gotten the best of the other.

Going tit for tat in an attempt to get even is insanity. Fighting fire with fire is at the heart of revenge and it only serves to keep tempers flared up. Youth that have no sense of boundaries will go get uncles, brothers, sisters or guns to get even with you in the name of revenge. The one sure remedy to revenge is to simply stop it. An opposing force must raise up to stop the rage of revenge before someone ends up dead or in jail. This opposing force is what is known as maturity. It takes a mature person to admit wrong doing, ask for forgiveness, give forgiveness or simply to walk away. What youth need to understand is: the bigger person is the one who has the maturity to walk away. Conflict that can't be ended by talking it out, needs to be ended by the smarter one walking out.

Physics teaches us that what goes in motion stays in motion until it meets with the force of opposition. Make the decision today to be that opposition. You must be a calmer person, cool headed and in control enough to find another way to solve your differences with others, instead of participating in vengeful actions that cause more harm. Don't be afraid or hesitant to act because of what you think others might say about you or the names they may

Forgiveness / Revenge

call you. Always remember, it's not what people call you that matters, it's what you answer to that does.

Forgiveness / Revenge

Forgiveness

Real Talk

It was a party like all other parties in Minnesota in 1993 when Laramiun Byrd was shot to death by a teenager named, Oshea Israel. The two got into an argument at the party and Oshea shot Laramiun to death. Once arraigned, Oshea was tried as an adult and convicted of murder. Subsequently, he was sentenced to twenty-five and a half years in prison. During the time that Oshea was locked down Mary Johnson, entered into his reality. Mary Johnson was the mother of Laramiun Byrd. She felt whoever this "animal" was needed to be caged and get whatever he had coming to him. She got permission from Stillwater State Prison officials to visit with Oshea. It was her hope to see if there was some kind of way she could forgive this young man for killing her son. Mary went to visit Oshea who, of course, was not expecting what kind of relationship would follow after that.

Mary found it in her heart to forgive her son's killer and continued to visit Oshea while he was in prison. She even found the heart to build a close relationship with him. She said she treated him as though he had never harmed her before. Finally, Oshea did

Forgiveness / Revenge

seventeen of the twenty-five and a half year prison sentence and was released. Mary Johnson, a shining example of forgiveness talked to her landlord and arranged to have Oshea stay next door to her in the same building. Oshea moved next door to her and today the two still have a relationship. Oshea speaks publicly about forgiveness in churches, jails and schools because Mary Johnson taught him how it feels to be forgiven by her very personal example. Could you have shown forgiveness, if this were your story?

Forgivenes

Self Evaluation

Circle One: True or False

True/False It is hard for me to forgive.

True/False I still hold some grudges about people that hurt me a few years ago.

True/False I can forgive once but not twice.

True/False Getting even with someone gives me satisfaction.

True/False I don't know how to forgive.

True/False I have never felt forgiven for what I have done to people.

True/False When someone apologizes for wronging me I can't seem to get it out of my head.

True/False I don't know how to forgive myself.

True/False Someone who walks away from confrontation is a coward.

True/False There is no such thing as walking away.

Forgiveness / Revenge

Forgiveness

Group Talk

Do you feel when you forgive another person you are letting them off the hook?

Should you forgive someone who is not sorry for what they have done?

Do we have to forgive people that use us over and over again?

Why do some people take a long time to forgive?

How do you know if you have forgiven another person?

What are ways that we can forgive ourselves for wrongs?

Is it right to forgive someone on conditions?

What are some ways that conflict can be solved without revenge? Give Examples.

blurb.com